THE METAPHYSICS OF GENDER

THE METAPHYSICS
OF GENDER

CHARLOTTE WITT

OXFORD
UNIVERSITY PRESS

OXFORD
UNIVERSITY PRESS

Oxford University Press, Inc., publishes works that further
Oxford University's objective of excellence
in research, scholarship, and education.

Oxford   New York
Auckland   Cape Town   Dar es Salaam   Hong Kong   Karachi
Kuala Lumpur   Madrid   Melbourne   Mexico City   Nairobi
New Delhi   Shanghai   Taipei   Toronto

With offices in
Argentina   Austria   Brazil   Chile   Czech Republic   France   Greece
Guatemala   Hungary   Italy   Japan   Poland   Portugal   Singapore
South Korea   Switzerland   Thailand   Turkey   Ukraine   Vietnam

Published by Oxford University Press, Inc.
198 Madison Avenue, New York, New York 10016

www.oup.com

Oxford is a registered trademark of Oxford University Press

ISBN 978-0-19-974040-6, pbk; 978-0-19-974041-3 hardcover.

A copy of this book's Cataloging-in-Publication Data is on file
with the Library of Congress.

Printed in the United States of America
on acid-free paper

For Anna Witt

CONTENTS

ACKNOWLEDGMENTS

The ideas in this book developed over a number of years, and benefited from discussion with colleagues at the Workshop on Gender and Philosophy and the philosophy departments at the University of New Hampshire and Dartmouth College. I would like to thank Willem deVries and Lynne Rudder Baker for their useful written comments on an earlier version of this manuscript. My students in the Self Seminar of 2010 gave me generous and thoughtful responses to the ideas in this book. I would like to thank the American Council of Learned Societies for supporting this scholarship with a Fellowship in 2003, and for inviting me to present my research at their Annual Meeting in 2005. I would also like to thank the College of Liberal Arts at the University of New Hampshire for research time supported by the Faculty Scholars Program in 2006.

I owe a particular debt of gratitude to two people who provided encouragement for my ideas about gender essentialism at a time when both the topic and my approach to it might have seemed perverse and unlikely of completion. It is always important to feel you have an audience—even a very small audience. Sally Haslanger has been a constant source of inspiration and support to me as I worked out the details of my view, which does not mean, of course, that she shares it. She is the best kind of philosophical friend. Mark Okrent has supported my work on this book with great personal generosity and philosophical insight, and I am deeply grateful to him.

PREFACE:

Why Gender Essentialism?

> The only dependable test for gender is the truth of a person's life, the lives we live each day.
> —(Jennifer Finney Boylan, "The XY Games,"
> New York Times, 8/03/08)

While working on this book, I have had occasion to try to explain its topic to friends, family, and acquaintances. I would ask whether they thought they would be the same person or individual if they were a different gender. All the people I spoke with thought that they would not be the same person if they were a different gender; the world, it seems, is filled with gender essentialists. Indeed, my interlocutors often had difficulty understanding why someone would write a book on a question that had an obvious answer. They may have also had doubts about my authorial competence once I explained that I had difficulty understanding the question much less answering it. This book is simply my attempt to articulate what they understand already. What does it mean to think that gender is essential to an individual, and why might it be true—at least for one understanding of gender, one interpretation of essentialism, and one kind of individual?

I have also on occasion explained or presented my research to colleagues in philosophy and in feminism/gender studies; they have, predictably, reacted very differently. I rarely find a professional colleague who thinks the question about his or her gender has an obvious and easy answer. And even when the question does seem easy to answer, there is skepticism about the relationship between that answer and gender essentialism. Sometimes the question itself, and the issue I use it to introduce, inspires a negative reaction. Feminists object to gender essentialism for many reasons: it is exclusionary, incompatible with social and political change, and reactionary. Other colleagues in philosophy add that it is false either as a claim about gender in particular, or for the same reasons that any essentialist theory is false. Still others doubt that it is an issue worthy of philosophical attention and should therefore be relegated to Women's Studies.

It is hard to resist thinking about a question that both has an obvious answer and ought not be asked, that is both politically suspect and not a philosophical question at all. More seriously, I have been drawn to work on gender essentialism for several reasons that are probably inextricably interwoven: a desire for clarity and understanding of what essentialist claims about gender might mean, a commitment to honor and to understand our ordinary day-to-day intuitions about gender, and a desire to contribute to ways of thinking useful to feminism. My work has been made possible by the thought of other feminists including especially those who are critical of essentialist theories about gender, which I am unable to discuss here in the detail they deserve.

Most feminist writing on gender essentialism, including critical work, focuses on the issue of whether there is some property common to all women, possession of which is necessary and sufficient for kind membership. Some feminists are skeptical that there is such a property. Others find the whole enterprise theoretically misguided and politically dangerous. In response, some feminists argue that political solidarity requires some commonality among all women, and there has been a revival of attempts to formulate a theoretical basis for solidarity. Let's call this the debate between gender realists and gender nominalists.

My focus is different. I am interested in the centrality of gender in our individual lived experiences, and I develop a framework for articulating that centrality. The framework I propose is essentialist, but not in a way that blocks social and political change. On the contrary, I hope that by articulating the pervasive and systematic gendering of our social lives, I will have helped to make visible the social reality that needs to change.

In this book I develop the claim that gender is uniessential to social individuals. There are two phases to my project. In the first three chapters, I explain, clarify, and defend the terms I use to express gender essentialism. I use an Aristotelian model to express unification essentialism (or uniessentialism). And I differentiate uniessentialism from other kinds of essentialist views (chapter 1). I define gender difference in terms of the socially mediated reproductive (or engendering) functions of women and men, and I develop an ascriptive theory of social normativity (chapter 2). Next, I distinguish between human organisms, social individuals, and persons and I argue that the claim of gender essentialism is best formulated as a claim about social individuals rather than about persons or about human organisms (chapter 3). Then, I construct an argument for the claim that gender is uniessential to social individuals and I discuss the similarities and differences between gender uniessentialism and other theories of gender essentialism (chapter 4). Finally, I discuss the normative situation of the self and the ontology of the self (chapter 5). In the Epilogue I briefly explore the consequences of gender uniessentialism for feminist politics.

One significant limitation of my argument is its scope. I do not argue here against feminists and other metaphysicians who reject essentialism of any stripe, concerning any and every kind of object. Rather, I focus on the question of *gender* essentialism on the assumption that essentialism of some stripe might be true of some kinds of objects. So, I do not address the broad scope anti-essentialist arguments concerning the instability of language made by some postmodern feminists or the arguments of philosophers, who follow Quine in rejecting "Aristotelian essentialism." There are two reasons for my decision to limit the scope of my project. The first is that it would simply be too huge a task to try to address all of the important anti-essentialist arguments of the twentieth century. It is quite enough to address those who might accept essentialism about the physical world, for example, but have questions about its extension to social reality, including social roles like gender. The second reason is that the relatively narrow focus of my argument allows me to highlight the issues that surround the notion of gender essentialism in particular, which I hope will make this book useful to philosophers who are interested in feminism and social justice.

THE METAPHYSICS OF GENDER

TWO NOTIONS OF ESSENCE

WHEN A COLLEAGUE INVITED me to teach the material in this chapter to his class of undergraduate philosophy majors, I began by asking them to write brief answers to two questions: First, are there any properties that define membership in the kind woman or the kind man? Second, would you be the same individual if you were gendered differently? The first question received a range of answers, from those who confidently singled out a physical or psychological property common to all women or to all men to those who hesitated, perhaps having been instructed on the moral and political failings of "essentialist" or "identity" thinking in another philosophy class. The second question prompted a lively discussion about gender, transgendered individuals, the relation between gender and self-understanding, and the ways in which our daily lives and activities are gendered. Speculations about universally shared properties, and doubts about whether there are any led the conversation in one direction. Reflections about the ways in which our lives and social roles (student, professor, mother, child) are inflected by our gender took the conversation in another. In this chapter I argue that my students were wrestling with two different notions of essence that address two different philosophical questions.[1]

---

1. My claim that gender is essential to social individuals has three terms needing explanation. In this chapter I describe the notion of essence that I will be using, but in the course of doing so I will necessarily use the other two terms, which I describe sequentially in chapters 2 (gender) and 3 (social individual). I hope that the sequential process of setting out the terms of my argument is not too confusing to the reader.

One difficulty facing discussions of gender essentialism is the lack of clarity in the terms of the conversation. So, what do I mean by essentialism? This chapter contains my answer to this question. I begin by distinguishing between kind and individual essentialism, a distinction that roughly corresponds to the two questions I posed to the students. Essentialism about a kind holds that there is a property or properties definitive of membership in that kind. Essentialism about an individual holds that there is a property or properties that make that individual the individual it is. In this book I focus on individual essentialism applied to gender. A further distinction is required, however, to sort out different versions of individual essentialism, namely, to distinguish Aristotle's unification essentialism from Kripke's identity essentialism.

Following my preliminary taxonomy of essentialisms, I focus in on individual essentialism in its Aristotelian guise. I explain how and why I use Aristotle's unification essentialism (or *uniessentialism* for short) to express gender essentialism. I then revisit identity essentialism and consider the way some philosophers use it to discuss issues of gender (and race) essentialism. The purpose of this section is to clarify the differences between uniessentialism and identity essentialism in relation to the topic of gender essentialism.

Finally, it is useful to round out my taxonomy of essentialisms by considering Locke's distinction between nominal and real essences. As I mentioned in the Preface, feminist debate concerning essentialism frequently turns on disagreement between gender nominalists and gender realists, and the concepts framing this debate originate with Locke. Some feminists have argued for adopting a theory of nominal essences about gender (Fuss 1989, de Lauretis 1994). Others are gender realists (Haslanger 2000, Zack 2005). As it turns out, however, the realism/nominalism debate among feminists is tangential to the focus of this book since it concerns the basis for membership in gender kinds, and not what makes an individual be the individual that it is.

A BRIEF TAXONOMY OF ESSENTIALISMS

Traditionally the notion of essence has had two different applications. First, we can think about essences in relation to kinds, and we can ask whether a collection of individuals constitutes a kind that is defined by a common and unique property (or properties). An essence in this sense is a property that determines kind membership.[2] In addition, some theories add the requirement that essential properties have causal or explanatory power.[3] Kinds defined by properties that meet the second requirement are sometimes called "natural kinds" because standard examples of natural kinds include biological species and material substances like water.[4] For convenience, let us call essentialism about kinds and the criteria for kind membership, *kind essentialism*.

A second notion of essence is that of a property or characteristic that makes an individual the individual that it is. An essence in this sense is a special kind of property of an individual; the property is necessary, or it tells us what the individual is fundamentally.[5] Let us call this type of essentialism,

2. I differentiate here among collections (e.g., the objects in my garage) that are arbitrary groupings of things, kinds (e.g., red things) that are groupings based on a property that defines its members, and natural kinds (e.g., biological species) that are kinds based on a non-arbitrary, explanatory or causal property. These are not uncontroversial distinctions but since I am not developing a theory of kind essentialism, they are not central to my purpose and I won't say more about them.

3. Nominal essences, which I discuss at the end of this chapter, do not have causal or explanatory power.

4. Dupre (1993) is critical of the view that biological species are natural kinds.

5. For a discussion of the difference between a modal conception of essentialism, in which the notion of a necessary property is basic, and a conception of an essence that answers the question "what is it?" see Fine (1994).

individual essentialism. The question—What makes an individual the individual it is?—can be understood in at least two ways, and the two interpretations yield slightly different theories of individual essentialism.

The first way, which yields a view I call *uniessentialism,* originates with Aristotle. For Aristotle the question "what is it?" asked of an individual substance expands into a question about the unity and organization of material parts into a new individual. He asks: Why do these materials constitute a house? And the answer is that they realize the functional property that defines being a house, which is to shelter humans and animals. Being a shelter for humans and animals is what makes these materials a house rather than a heap of stuff or a sum of parts. The house functional property explains why a new, unified individual exists at all.

The second interpretation, which yields a view I call *identity essentialism,* is associated with Kripke (1977, 1980). For Kripke the question—What makes an individual be the individual it is?—concerns the identity of the individual. What makes this lectern the very individual it is (as opposed to some other lectern)? One answer is that it must be made from the very materials from which it, in fact, originated. If it had originated from a different piece of wood then it would not be this very lectern. Its origins are a necessary property of the lectern. Notice that its material origins are not an essential property of the house on the Aristotelian (or unification) understanding of essential property. Hence there is reason to think that these are two different theories of individual essentialism in the sense that they respond to different questions about individuals. Aristotle explains why a new individual exists at all over and above the sum of its material constituents or parts. In contrast, Kripke begins with an existing individual, and asks about which of that individual's properties are necessary to be that very individual.

Let us now look at several feminist arguments against kind and individual essentialism applied to gender. While I do not think that these anti-essentialist arguments are successful, they provide a useful bridge between my taxonomy of essentialisms and feminist discussions of gender essentialism. Many feminists deny that women (and men) are kinds whose members share a defining property, and they reject gender essentialism understood as a claim about kind membership.[6] In other words, they reject gender realism. Since women (and men) form social kinds or groups, not natural kinds, their membership cannot be defined by a shared property.[7] This argument assumes that only membership in natural kinds (like biological species) could be defined by a common property because only natural kinds are stable and homogenous.[8] In contrast, the features that characterize women (and men) vary over time and across different cultures and, as a result, there are no features that are common to all women (or to all men). There is also variation within a single culture due to the intersection of gender with other social identities, like race, or class (Spelman 1988). So, even within one culture, there is no possibility of a shared feature or features common to all women or to all men that determine kind membership.[9] Those who would advocate gender essentialism understood as kind essentialism mistake what is social and variable

6. Recently, some feminists have defended realism about gender, using a variety of different theories of kinds, and a variety of different definitions of gender (Haslanger 2000, Zack 2005, Alcoff 2006).

7. This argument assumes a distinction between sex and gender that has been controversial in feminist theory. I discuss the distinction between sex and gender in chapter 2.

8. In "Social Roles, Social Construction and Stability," Ron Mallon argues for the stability of social kinds (Schmitt 2003).

9. The second feature of essential properties, their causal or explanatory role, is not central to feminist criticisms of gender essentialism. Since anti-essentialist feminists tend to argue against the claim that there is any property common to all women, this condition will receive most of my attention in what follows.

for what is natural and fixed. I call this *the social construction argument* against gender essentialism (Witt 1995). Further, given the variability of women, kind essentialism will necessarily marginalize and exclude some women by defining kind membership using properties that they do not have. I call this *the exclusion argument* against gender essentialism (Witt 1995).

Although individual essentialism is less prominent in feminist discussions of gender essentialism than kind essentialism, there is reason to think that many feminists would reject it as well. One objection might be that it runs counter to the correct view of the self as a subject that chooses, negotiates, rejects, or performs identities like gender. In this view, nothing *makes* the individual man or woman the individual that he or she is, because the identities and self-understandings that make up our social selves are chosen, negotiated, performed, rejected, and so on. Those who would advocate gender essentialism according to the second notion, therefore, are mistaking subjects or selves for objects or things—with serious consequences for the possibility of women's agency (including their political activity), women's autonomy, and women's freedom (Butler 1997, Alcoff 2006). I call this the ontological argument against individual essentialism about gender because mistaking self-determining subjects or agents for causally determined objects is an ontological error.

I have described feminist arguments against kind and individual gender essentialism here primarily for purposes of orientation, and my response to them will be brief. I don't think that the social construction argument, the exclusion argument, and the ontological argument establish their conclusions. Let's begin with the social construction argument. The fact that an individual, institution, or kind has a social origin or social definition does not in and of itself rule out essentialism about that individual, institution, or kind (Witt 1995). Think of Aristotle's house or Kripke's lectern; the fact that they are artifacts does not rule out ipso facto that they might have essential properties. The social construction argument does not—in itself—establish anti-essentialism about gender.

The exclusion argument targets kind essentialism about gender because it holds that the properties proposed to define membership in gender kinds necessarily exclude some women and some men. My response is twofold. First, I will argue in a moment that individual and kind essentialism are, in principle, independent of one another, and so the conclusion of the exclusion argument, even if true, does not apply to individual essentialism, which is my focus. Second, it seems to me that the exclusion argument needs to be supplemented by some other theoretical notion, like that of intersectionality, in order to tell against kind essentialism about gender. Without a theory that shows exclusion to be the inevitable result of attempts to define membership in gender kinds, the exclusion argument works in a cautionary fashion to warn against hasty generalization or over-generalization. If that is right, then the exclusion argument—by itself—does not establish anti-essentialism (or anti-realism) about gender kinds (Mikkola 2006).

Finally, the ontological argument claims that individual essentialism treats subjects as objects and leaves no room for individual choice and agency. This criticism does not apply to the framework that I develop to articulate gender essentialism. In chapter 3 I introduce the notion of a social individual (or agent) who acts in and through her various social positions or social roles. I distinguish the agency of social individuals from the causal relations that govern objects. The beings that are essentially gendered are agents, and not objects. In chapter 2 I discuss the conditions governing social normativity, which are relevant to the question of individual freedom, and I argue that social recognition is a necessary element in social normativity. But social recognition is not a causal relationship, it does not transform social individuals into objects, and it does not impede agency. On the contrary, social recognition is a condition that enables agents to act in and through the social positions that they occupy.

Individual and kind essentialism are often not clearly distinguished by feminists who argue against gender essentialism (Stoljar 1995). And, as we have just seen, most feminist criticisms of gender essentialism are directed against kind essentialism (or gender realism). My interest in individual essentialism has several sources. First, because individual gender essentialism is relatively unexplored territory, it is still possible to say something interesting and useful about it. But another reason for my focus is that individual essentialism seems to express the centrality of gender in our lived experiences. Kind essentialism expresses the powerful political idea that I share something in common with all other women and provides a basis for political solidarity. But individual essentialism expresses the equally compelling idea that my gender is constitutive of my being the social individual that I am. As I noted in the Preface, most women and most men think it is simply obvious that their gender is inextricably interwoven in their social existences and identities. This intuition deserves exploration by feminists even though what it means is not clear or perhaps *because* what it means is not clear. Finally, it is individual essentialism, rather than kind essentialism that intersects with questions of agency, and the issue of agency is central to feminist theory. In chapter 5, I develop the notion of the self as an agent, who acts from a practical identity or social role, which connects the self to the social world and its available positions.

I use an Aristotelian model to express uniessentialism; the essence is the cause of being of the individual (Witt 1989). More precisely, its essence causes these materials or parts to constitute a new individual substance rather than a mere heap of stuff or collection of parts. In chapter 4 I argue that the numerous social positions that we occupy are systematically unified by our gender; hence, our gender is uniessential to us as social beings. The unity of social agents is not a relationship among material parts; it is a relationship of normative unity among our various social position occupancies. There is much more to say about the concept of normative unity, and I discuss it in some detail in chapter 4. In this chapter I concentrate on describing my model for uniessentialism, and explaining how it applies to gender.

I think that individual and kind essentialism are conceptually independent of one another. According to one interpretation of Aristotelian essentialism, however, the species form (e.g., the property of rationality) is both what grounds species or kind membership *and* what is essential to the existence of each individual (Spelman, 1988, Stoljar 1995, Alcoff 2006). This is not my interpretation of Aristotle's theory of form and essence (Witt 1989), but it is a common and traditional understanding of his view. So, in at least one important example, kind essentialism and uniessentialism are interconnected theories. If kind and individual essentialism were conceptually interdependent, then there would only be one view to discuss in which the essence is both a universal species form and the cause of being of individuals. But if, as I argue below, individual essentialism and kind essentialism are conceptually independent of one another and respond to different philosophical issues, then I will not need to defend kind essentialism about gender in order to make my case for individual essentialism.[10]

What is the relationship between individual and kind essentialism? I think that the two essentialisms are conceptually independent of one another. They are conceptually independent of one another because they address distinct philosophical questions. I focus here on the difference between uniessentialism and kind essentialism.

---

10. I distinguish the two essentialisms in order to define my project not because I think that kind essentialism about gender is mistaken.

To see that uniessentialism and kind essentialism are conceptually independent of one another, let us consider the example of a biological organism. We can ask two very different questions about it. First, what makes the organism an individual? An organism, like an animal or a cell, is a composite of many individual parts, and yet it is also a unified individual, not just a collection or sum of individuals or parts. What orders or organizes the individual parts so that they compose a unified individual? It seems that an adequate answer to this question must be a relational property that orders all of the individual parts into a functional unity, and that functional unity is an individual organism. The relational property is the uniessence of the organism; it is by virtue of realizing a particular function that the parts of an organism are unified into an individual. Its function is uniessential to the organism.

A different question is whether or not animals (i.e., individual organisms) should be grouped into species understood as natural kinds and, if they should, what the basis is for these groupings. This is to raise the issue of kind essentialism with respect to animals. The question of kind essentialism is not answered when we determine what is uniessential to an organism; it is a conceptually distinct question. Maybe organisms like animals should be grouped into natural kinds; but maybe not. Maybe they should be understood to form populations rather than natural kinds. Maybe species are individuals and their members (i.e., organisms) are parts of the individual. Questions like these about kinds are conceptually independent of the question of why an organism is a unified individual.[11] Of course, it might be that the feature that is uniessential to the organism also serves as the basis for its kind membership; my point is that it need not do so.

---

11. For a good discussion of the ontological status of species see Ereshefsky (2008).

I have used the example of biological organisms to illustrate the different questions raised by uniessentialism and kind essentialism and to show that the two essentialisms are conceptually independent of one another. We can draw a parallel distinction with regard to gender essentialism. The property or properties (if there are any) that are shared by all men or by all women and form the basis of gender kinds need not be uniessential to individual men or individual women. For example, it could be that the basis for grouping women as a class or kind is that they are recognized to have a certain reproductive function, and yet it might not be the case that any individual woman is a unified individual because of her gender. Aristotle differentiated between men and women (the male and the female) because of their different reproductive functions, but he did not think that either men or women were individuals because of their reproductive functions. Rather, he thought that both men and women were constituted as individuals by virtue of the presence of human soul (conceived of functionally) to their bodies. The human soul (conceived of functionally) is uniessential to both individual men and individual women; but men (as a kind) are defined in terms of the male reproductive function and women (as a kind) are defined in terms of the female reproductive function. Because uniessentialism and kind essentialism address different questions it is possible to develop an argument for unification gender essentialism that does not include an argument for kind gender essentialism.[12]

UNIESSENTIALISM AND GENDER

I am interested in the question of whether our gender (being a man, being a woman) is essential to us as social

12. It is also possible to show that identity essentialism is different from kind essentialism, but I will not pursue that issue here.

individuals.[13] To explore this issue I use an Aristotelian model to express gender essentialism. For Aristotle, the essence is the cause of being of the individual whose essence it is. Both artifacts and biological organisms have material parts that are organized into an individual that is not identical to the sum of its material parts. In both cases we can ask why the material parts constitute a new individual rather than a heap or a collection of parts. Hence both artifacts and biological organisms have essences in that they both have a principle that explains their existence as individuals. Artifacts and biological individuals are also similar because the principle that explains their existence as individuals is a functional essence. A functional essence is an essential property that explains what the individual is for, what its purpose is, and that organizes the parts toward that end. Of course, the origin of the purpose differs in the case of artifacts and natural beings. For artifacts, the purpose has an external origin in the intentions and purposes of human beings whereas the purposes of biological individuals are intrinsic to the organism.

It is important to be clear that the question of why a sum of parts makes up a new individual is not a causal question. To use Aristotle's idiolect, it is important to distinguish between the cause of being (ontological question) and the cause of becoming (causal question). One could ask, for example, about how a house is constructed out of building materials when that would be a question about the process of pouring concrete, building a

---

13. The framework I develop here could accommodate a third gender if that gender plays an analogous role in the social agency of some individuals as being a man or being a woman does in the agency of others. Transgendered individuals, for example, could have their social role occupancies organized by their gender; being transgendered could be the principle of normative unity that unites their social roles and positions. In chapter 2 I discuss two additional issues concerning multiple genders, namely the role of social recognition in establishing social position occupancy and the definition of gender.

frame, and so on. This is a causal question as the answer specifies the causal factors that produce an individual artifact (or an individual organism). The ontological question is not about the process of generation; rather, it focuses upon the existence of an individual, which is not simply the sum of its parts. What explains the existence of an individual? What accounts for the fact that it is an individual? It is also important to be clear that my use of an artifact to exemplify Aristotelian uniessentialism should not be taken to imply that uniessentialism is primarily a theory about artifacts, which I extend from its central case and apply to women and to men. Rather, uniessentialism is a theory about the ontological constitution of unified individuals, and it applies to any unified individual that is made up of parts, including artifacts, organisms, persons, agents, plays, God, and so on.

Here is the Aristotelian model exemplified by an artifact, a house. A sum of material parts that realizes the functional property or properties of a house is an individual house and its house functional property is essential to it. The functional properties of a house unify the building materials (or parts) into a new individual, a house. It is because these bricks and boards (or these windows and doors) realize the function of providing shelter to humans and animals that an individual house exists. If the very same parts were scattered across a junkyard (or neatly arranged at Lowe's) then they would not realize the house function (providing shelter, etc.) and a house would not exist. Its house functional properties are uniessential to the individual house. The essence explains why a collection of parts is unified into a new individual.

Uniessentialism is not kind essentialism. The two theories address different questions or problems, and the issues or problems are, in principle, independent of one another. Uniessentialism explains why an individual exists rather than a heap. For instance, the house functional properties explain why certain materials are an individual house rather than a mere heap (or some other artifact). Absent the house functional properties, we would not have an individual; we would have a collection of building materials. In parallel fashion we can ask why an individual organism exists (e.g., a human being) rather than a collection of parts (heart, lung, brain). The question of whether, and on what basis, artifacts like houses and natural beings, like organisms, are kinds is—in principle—a conceptually independent question. It may turn out, for example, that biological species are not natural kinds, and that kind essentialism does not hold of biological species, but that finding is—in principle—conceptually independent of the truth of uniessentialism applied to organisms.[14]

Uniessentialism is also not identity essentialism. Although the functional essence of the house explains why an individual exists (over and above its parts), it does not thereby secure its particular identity. As far as its function goes, it is just like the house next door. In contrast, identity essentialism asks what makes this individual the very individual it is. To be this very individual, a house must be made from the materials actually used to construct it. A human being must originate from the very sperm and egg from which she actually did originate; a lectern must be made from the very wood from which it was, in fact, made. Identity essentialism is also—in principle—independent from kind essentialism because it need not broach the question of artifactual or biological kinds in its investigation of individual identity.

Notice that the uniessential properties of the house are functional properties that are realized in and by its material parts. Functional properties are relational rather than intrinsic properties. A window serves its function in relation to the house

---

14. John Dupre (1993) argues that biological species are not natural kinds. And Eliot Sober (1990) argues that population thinking has replaced the notion of species in contemporary biology.

as a whole and its other components. Also, the functional properties of artifacts are always enmeshed in a broad social context of use. A house has the function of providing shelter but that function is embedded in various social practices (e.g., architecture), social structures (e.g., patriarchal households), and other conditions. And finally, functional properties have a normative dimension because the function specifies what that object ought to do, and not simply what it does. A house with a leaky roof is a house, even if it is defective in relation to its essential task of providing shelter. Because functional properties are normative, it is possible for an individual to have a function that it cannot or does not perform. A house that was flooded by Hurricane Katrina is a house even though it does not (and perhaps cannot) perform its function.

It might be useful at this point to draw a distinction between two levels of normativity that pertain to the functional properties of objects. At the first level, an individual can be judged as performing its function well or badly; and the function itself provides the norm of judgment. For example, we decide that a bank robber performs her job well (or badly) by looking at what the function of a bank robber is. If a robber is caught by the police or flees without money then she is a defective bank robber. However, at a second level we can evaluate the function itself, in terms of ethical, political, or religious norms, for example. In this case, the norm of evaluation is not determined by the function itself but by an external standard. This distinction will be important in chapter 2 because it will allow me to distinguish between the social norms that individual women and men are responsive to and evaluable under, and the value of the functions that ground those norms.

I underline these three features of functional properties looking forward to my discussion of gender in chapter 2. In that chapter I introduce the terminology of social positions (like being a parent or being a doctor) and social roles (the norms associated with social positions). I propose to define the social position of being a woman and being a man in terms of the socially mediated reproductive (or engendering) functions that an individual is recognized (by others) to perform. The engendering function, like the function of providing shelter, is a relational property (an individual serves that function only in relation to other individuals). Engendering is also a function that is realized in a social context of institutions, traditions, and the like. And, like other functional properties, engendering is normative; it describes what individuals who are women and men ought to do, and not what they actually do. Women and men are responsive to and evaluable under the social role associated with their respective social positions; but the engendering function and the social roles are themselves available for normative evaluation and critique.

Here is the application of Aristotle's model to gender. A social individual (or agent) occupies many social positions simultaneously (and many more diachronically) but its gender unifies the sum of social position occupancies into a new social individual. Its gender (being a man, being a woman) is uniessential to the social individual. It is worthwhile pausing here to provide a preliminary clarification of two important features of my application of unification essentialism to gender: (1) the claim that gender is uniessential to social individuals, and (2) the unifying role of gender.

My application of the Aristotelian model to gender uses the notion of a social individual and it is reasonable to wonder exactly what a social individual is. In chapter 3 I distinguish social individuals from both human organisms and persons. I define persons as those individuals who have a first-person perspective or have self-consciousness (Baker 2000). By human organisms I mean individuals who are members of the human species, who realize the human genotype or satisfy whatever other criteria are proposed to define membership in the human species. Not every member of the human species is a person (e.g., a baby) and, conversely, there could be persons who are not members of the human species. (Baker 2007a) Social individuals are those individuals who occupy social positions—indeed, multiple social positions—both synchronically and diachronically. Social individuals differ from human organisms because their actions are bound by social normativity, which is different from biological normativity in two respects. First, social norms are not species-based; they are flexible and variable and differ from culture to culture. Second, social normativity requires the recognition by others that an agent is both responsive to and evaluable under a social norm. Social individuals differ from persons in that they essentially exist in a web of social relations whereas persons do not. In chapter 3 I elaborate and defend these distinctions, and I argue that social individuals are the appropriate candidates for formulating the claim of gender essentialism.

Let us now consider the second point in need of clarification. In the case of an artifact, the functional essence unifies the material parts into an individual. It is because the building materials are unified and organized so as to realize that property of being a shelter for humans that an individual house exists. But what does the gender functional essence unify in order to constitute a social individual? And what notion of unity is relevant? Social individuals occupy multiple social positions synchronically and diachronically. At any given moment, a social individual occupies multiple positions—professor, parent, and so on—and the question is what unites those social position occupancies so that a social individual exists? How are they unified and organized? A bundle of social position occupancies is not an individual, just as a heap of house parts is not an individual. I argue in chapter 4 that our gender is a pervasive and fundamental social position that unifies and determines all other social positions both synchronically and diachronically. It unifies them not physically, but by providing a principle of normative unity. It is as a woman that I am a parent or a professor (or whatever the full range of my social roles might be at the moment or over time). In chapter 4 I will have more to say about normative unity and why social individuals need a principle of normative unity.

In this chapter, however, I am simply interested in describing unification essentialism applied to gender and distinguishing it from other ways of expressing gender essentialism. I will not give any reason or argument to believe that it is true or even plausible. Rather, my goal is to introduce the Aristotelian model as a way of thinking about—or expressing—individual gender essentialism. To continue with the description of uniessentialism and its application to gender, it is useful to contrast it with identity essentialism, and the application of identity essentialism to gender and to race.

IDENTITY ESSENTIALISM AND GENDER

Identity essentialism is intimately connected with modality; an individual's essential properties are its necessary properties. Moreover, Kripke's views on individual essences are articulated within the semantic framework of a theory of reference for proper names. According to Kripke, proper names do not have meanings or senses, but rather refer directly to individuals. Both the details of this theory and its application to kind terms (tiger) and substance terms (water) are beyond the scope of this discussion. Kripke frames the question of the essences of individuals as follows:

> Here is a lectern. A question which has often been raised in philosophy is: What are its essential properties? What properties,

aside from trivial ones like self-identity are such that this object has to have them if it exists at all, are such that if an object did not have it, it would not be this object?[15]

In this text Kripke raises the question of the essential features of individuals, what I call individual essentialism.[16] It is important to see that Kripke is not asking us to imagine what changes an artifact like the lectern could undergo and still persist. Rather than thinking temporally about change, we are to think modally, about possibility and necessity. The properties an object *must* have if it exists at all are the properties that, if the object did not have them, it would not be that very object. Kripke classifies the necessary properties of individuals into three sorts: properties of origin (a material object must come from the very hunk of matter it did come from), sortal properties (being a lectern is a necessary property of a lectern), properties of substance (a material object must be made from the kind of matter it is in fact made from). In another text, Kripke discusses the example of the Queen of England and says that the necessary property of origin is the very sperm and egg from which, in fact, the Queen originated (Kripke 1980). In biological individuals, the necessity of origins is identified with the original genetic materials, the sperm and egg.

As we have just seen, unification essentialism is not formulated using modal notions (possibility, necessity).[17] Further,

---

15. "Identity and Necessity" in Schwartz (1977), p. 86.
16. Kripke (1980) is also interested in the essential features of kinds (like tiger) and stuffs (like water).
17. A separate issue is whether Aristotle's uniessentialism supports modal claims. It seems to me that it does support contrary to fact statements of potentiality or possibility like, If the wooden parts did not have the function of a house then they would not constitute a house. But the central focus of Aristotle's theory of essence is the role essences play in the organization and unity of substances and not the relationship between essences and modality. For a contemporary discussion of the difference between Aristotelian essentialism and contemporary modal essentialism see Fine (1994).

unlike Kripke's theory, it does not depend upon any particular semantics for those notions or for names and natural kind terms. Unification essentialism is not constructed out of the same theoretical ingredients as Kripke's theory (Witt 1989, Charles 2002). The basic difference, however, concerns what issue the theories address. Unification essentialism asks why a hunk of matter or an assemblage of material parts constitutes an individual. Why does an individual exist at all, over and above a collection of parts? In contrast, Kripke asks of an individual which of its properties it must have to be that very individual. What properties must an individual have to be this very individual, that same individual? Although both questions are about individuals and not kinds, they are not the very same questions. For convenience I refer to Kripke's essentialism as identity essentialism, because it uses our intuitions concerning the identity of individuals to determine what their essential properties are.

Some philosophers use Kripke's identity essentialism to explore essentialism about race or gender (Appiah 1990, Stoljar 1995, Zack 1996). Appiah, for example, explicitly couches his reflections on race, sex, and gender in relation to Kripke's theory. Appiah begins by distinguishing between questions of metaphysical or biological identity, and questions of ethical identity. Our metaphysical or biological identity is what Kripke was talking about in holding that human beings necessarily come from the very same sperm and egg we actually came from (the necessity of origin applied to biological beings). In this metaphysical/biological context, if I originated from genetic material with XX chromosomes, then, given the necessity of origin, I would not be me unless I was genetically female.[18] We can

---

18. Appiah acknowledges that this is an oversimplification of the biological facts. Human sexual identity is determined using several criteria, which do not always line up with one another. For a discussion, see Fausto-Sterling (2000).

contrast the biological determinations of female and male with the social roles of being a woman or being a man. It is possible for a biological female to live as a man or a biological male to live as a woman.[19] In relation to this distinction, Appiah introduces the notion of the ethical self. "As many think of them, sex—female and male, the biological statuses—and gender—masculine and feminine, the social roles—provide the sharpest model for a distinction between the metaphysical notion of identity that goes with Kripkean theorizing and the notion of identity—the ethical notion—that I am seeking to explore" (Appiah 1997, p. 77). The ethical self is an individual with projects and a self-conception. In the ethical context, when we ask the question "But would it still be me?" the answer reflects our self-conception as social agents rather than an external metaphysical/scientific truth like the necessity of origin or the biological determination of sex. Appiah thinks that a change in his gender would usher into existence a new ethical self, whereas a change in his race would not.

I have described Appiah's views in some detail, not so much to take issue with them, but rather to explain that I will not be developing individual essentialism about gender along the lines that he pursues. As Appiah sees it, the question of gender essentialism is a question about an individual's ethical or pragmatic self-conception. My approach differs from Appiah's because I do not think that the question of gender essentialism is fundamentally a question about an individual's self-conception. Rather, as I explain in chapter 5, I think that our self-conceptions or practical identities are formed in relation to the social positions that we occupy, and my focus is on the way that our social position occupancies are unified and organized. I think that there is an important, ontological

19. The sex/gender distinction is introduced in chapter 2. For examples of the multiple ways that one's sex can diverge from one's gender, see Dreger (1998).

question about the unity of the social individual that is prior to, and independent of, how we understand ourselves. Uniessentialism is a theory that explains how a collection of parts is unified so that a new individual exists, but Appiah's identity approach takes the individual (whether the metaphysical/biological human organism or the ethical self) as a given, and then asks what conditions must be met to be that very individual. This is an important and interesting project, but it is not my project. In the Preface to this book I explained how I introduced its topic by asking friends and acquaintances whether they thought they would be the same individual if they changed gender. This is Appiah's question; it addresses the centrality of gender in our practical self-conceptions. Although I think this is a useful question to orient the reader to the general topic of my book, and I don't doubt that, for many of us, our gender is central to our practical identities, this claim is not a premise of my argument for gender uniessentialism.

Some feminists think that Locke's theory of nominal essences provides an account of the meaning of gender terms that is preferable to the Aristotelian approach (Battersby 1998, Alcoff 2006). For that reason Locke is an important figure in the feminist debates over gender essentialism, and I end this chapter's taxonomy of essentialisms with a consideration of his theory in relation to the distinction between individual and kind essentialism.

NOMINAL AND REAL ESSENCES

For Locke, the topic of essence arises in his account of language, and in particular, in his account of how we classify individuals into kinds or species. A nominal essence is an abstract idea that corresponds to the meaning of a general word, like "tiger" or "water." Linguistic meanings are conventional for

Locke and consist of the collection of ideas associated with a word: water is liquid, clear, refreshing, and so on. Nominal essences are the general ideas that correspond to the terms that we use for classification. A real essence, in contrast, is the material composition—or minute parts—of an object that causes us to perceive it as we do. Real essences are, in principle, unknowable by us since they are the causes of—but not part of—our perceptual experiences that are recorded in the nominal essence. We know they are there, but, according to Locke, we don't know what they are. We might think of the atomic structure of water as H2O as corresponding to Locke's real essence, keeping in mind that he did not think that the material structure was knowable.

Pretty clearly, Locke's theory of nominal essences pertains to kinds and not individuals. The theory is his response to the traditional interpretation of Aristotle's doctrine of species forms that are both essential to individuals and the basis for their kind membership. For Locke, in contrast, the nominal essence is an abstract general idea, which we use to classify individuals. There are, of course, many possible ways to classify individuals, and our minds are actively engaged in forming the abstract general ideas that we use to categorize particulars. Locke's theory of nominal essences is a theory of kind essentialism that does not posit any form or feature of the individual that is both essential to it and the basis for its kind membership. Hence, Locke provides the theoretical framework for those feminists who are gender nominalists.

Natalie Stoljar suggests that there is not a sharp distinction between nominal and real essence for social terms like "woman": "For social concepts, the real essence is constituted by the social features of the world given in the definition of the term" (1995, p. 278). For social terms, in effect, there are only nominal essences. Stoljar is critical of the utility of a nominal essence of "woman" for feminist purposes because a nominal essence introduces a social universal "woman" that ignores the real differences among women of different social classes, races, and so on.

The upshot of this very brief discussion of Locke's nominal essences is that they pertain to kind essentialism and not individual essentialism. Following Stoljar's suggestion, we can bracket the issue of real essences (in the Lockean sense) for social kinds. Those feminists who advocate nominal essentialism about gender are proposing a theory of kind essentialism. Since my primary interest here is in individual essentialism, Locke's theory of nominal essences and its value for feminism is tangential to my central focus.

The purpose of this chapter has been to clarify the type of gender essentialism that is the topic of this book. In that regard, it has been important to distinguish between individual and kind essentialism. And it has also been important to explain in some detail the difference between uniessentialism and identity essentialism, and to introduce the Aristotelian model I will be using in relation to gender. But there is still more to say about the framework that I will be using to articulate gender essentialism. In particular, I need to say more about social individuals, how they differ from persons and human organisms, and I need to make a case for the relevance of social individuals for questions of gender essentialism. It is also necessary to say more about the functional notion of gender that my argument employs, and why it is a useful way to think about gender. In the next chapter I discuss the project of defining gender in terms of the different socially mediated reproductive (or engendering) functions of men and women. Chapter 3 defines social individuals and differentiates them from both persons and human organisms. I also explain why gender essentialism is best expressed in relation to social individuals, rather than in relation to human organisms or persons.

GENDER AND SOCIAL

NORMATIVITY

IMAGINE A HUMAN CULTURE in which the physical trait of height was socially significant, and people in that culture were divided into Talls and Shorts. The presence of people at the margins of this distinction did not affect its social significance, and there were arbitrary rules, and even physical interventions, that pushed people of average height in one direction or the other. This was done for their own good. Some rebels refused to identify as either Tall or Short, and they walked on tiptoe or with bent knees to parody and destabilize the culture's height hegemonies. Some rebels also posed intellectual difficulties by pointing out that the designations "Tall" and "Short," although apparently labels for intrinsic, physical characteristics of individuals, were actually culturally variable terms that encoded and reinforced cultural norms.[1] Imagine further that necessary social functions in this culture were shaped by elaborate norms reflecting the distinction between Talls and Shorts. Dining is one example. Talls always ate before Shorts, who served them and then ate what was left. Perhaps this set of dining norms originated because the Talls were bigger than the Shorts; perhaps the norms were thought to make sense because the Shorts were closer to the table, and hence it was easier and more natural

1. My daughter Anna, who at five feet tall is considered a short American woman, would not be short in her country of origin, Vietnam. Being tall and being short are relational properties, and one of the relata is the social context within which the properties are attributed.

27

for them to place items on the table. Maybe it was the psychology of the Shorts, who after all were servile, that explained the apparent solidity and good sense of the social practice. Perhaps there was a religious justification in that their deity, the Giant, resembled Talls more than Shorts. Maybe the dining roles persisted because of the common understanding that Talls needed more food than Shorts and had difficulty controlling their impulses. Without the existing dining norms the Talls might simply take the food from the Shorts and not even leave them leftovers, so the social norms governing dining were truly in the best interests of everyone. Since their science, religion, and politics served to reinforce the height-based social hierarchy, its contingency and its unfairness were largely invisible both to Talls and to Shorts.

There is significant overlap between women and men on a broad range of intellectual, psychological, and physical characteristics, and also significant differences among men and among women (Rhode 1997). Any attempt to define being a woman and being a man in terms of these kinds of properties will fail because of individual human variation. And, as I explain below, while sexual morphology and other biological markers provide a basis for distinguishing male from female human beings (although not all humans are either male or female), it is not necessary that an individual satisfy the criteria for being male to be a man or the criteria for being female to be a woman. To underscore this point I will introduce a distinction between sex and gender, using "male" and "female" to refer to sex and "man" and "woman" to refer to gender. But if we can't use either intrinsic physical or psychological properties or sexual morphology and other biological criteria to distinguish women and men, how can we even meaningfully express the claim of gender essentialism?

My parable of the Talls and the Shorts suggests a different direction, which is to define being a woman and being a man in relation to a necessary social function. Let me introduce some useful terminology. Being a Short and being a Tall are examples of social positions, which we will imagine are defined in relation to the social function of dining. For example, to be a Tall is to eat first, and to be a Short is to serve food to the Talls. A social role refers to the norms associated with a social position. Note that the Short's norm of servility is not directly required by their dining protocol although we can see that the norm both serves and reinforces that protocol. Further, in Height Society an individual is responsive to and evaluable under a social role by virtue of occupying a social position. A Short, for example, is responsive to and evaluable under the norm of eating leftovers at meals simply by virtue of being a Short. And finally, whether a given individual is a Short does not depend upon that individual's self-understanding or practical identification as a Short but rather on social recognition of that individual as a Short.

Following the example of Height Society, I define the social positions of being a man and being a woman in terms of the different socially mediated reproductive functions of men and women. The social positions of being a man and being a woman have elaborate social roles (or sets of norms) only some of which are directly associated with their reproductive functions. Women and men are responsive to their gendered social roles and evaluable by others in relation to those roles just by virtue of their social position occupancy. And whether an individual is a woman or a man is fixed by the reproductive role that individual is recognized by others to perform. Social recognition is a necessary condition for occupying gendered social positions. The social recognition of an individual's gender is complex and culturally variable. It includes, but is not limited to, recognition by other members of the social group; institutional recognition as exemplified by birth certificates, driver's licenses, marriage licenses; other forms of group recognition such as initiation rituals. The content of gendered social roles is also culturally relative and varies historically. I propose a functional definition of gender in part because of the evident inadequacy of basing gender difference on the intellectual, psychological and physical differences between women and men, but primarily because a functional definition of gender fits into the framework I use to express gender essentialism.

I argue in this book that gender is uniessential to social individuals. Each term in this claim is conceptually linked to the others. For example, the definition of gender that I develop in this chapter fits with the notion of essentialism that I introduced in chapter 1. Uniessentialism is the view that an essence organizes and unifies a collection of materials (or parts) into a new individual. A uniessence is explanatory; it explains the existence of the new individual as a unity and not just a sum of material parts. Aristotle's primary examples are artifacts and organisms, and the essential properties that unify individual artifacts and individual organisms are functional properties. It is because these boards and bricks realize the house function that an individual house exists over and above the sum of its parts. Functional properties unify and determine the parts so that a new individual exists. If we think about an individual's gender as a social position that is functionally defined, we can follow the Aristotelian model in articulating the claim of gender essentialism.

In chapter 3 I introduce the notion of a social individual and distinguish social individuals from human organisms and from persons. I argue that the question of gender essentialism is appropriately raised of social individuals and not of human organisms or persons. There is a conceptual connection between the definition of gender I develop in this chapter and the kind of individuals that are gendered. The conceptual connection between gender and social individuals is made via the notion of social normativity. Human reproductive functioning can be considered from two perspectives. As a biological function, human reproduction has a normative component. Our organs and parts can function as they should or fail to function as they should; they have the normativity common to all biological functions. This biological normativity is species based; it is as a member of the human species that our biological functions are fixed.[2]

As a socially mediated function, however, human reproduction has a second layer of normativity—social normativity—which is specified in a culture's norms and expectations. The gendered social roles that are defined in relation to reproduction are not determined by species membership alone, and they vary widely in different cultures and in different historical periods. Moreover, social recognition is an intrinsic ingredient in social normativity (but not in biological normativity) because of the role played by social recognition in the determination of an individual's social position occupancy. I argue in chapter 3 that gender is appropriately attributed to social individuals rather than human organisms because the roles attaching to women and men by virtue of their social position occupancy are expressions of social normativity. The definition of essentialism I use, the notion of gender I develop, and the individuals who, I will argue, are essentially gendered are interrelated concepts and not stand-alone ideas. When I say that gender is essential to social individuals, I am making a claim that uses the notion of uniessentialism, of gender defined in terms of socially mediated reproductive functions, and of social individuals.

2. The existence of biological normativity is debated in the philosophy of biology and I do not intend to enter into that debate. I think there are good reasons to endorse biological norms, but that is not part of my argument here. My point can be read hypothetically: If biological normativity exists, then social normativity differs from it in important ways. It is important to underline the difference between social and biological normativity because there is a strong tendency to conflate the two and to think that the norms associated with engendering are substantially biological.

In this chapter I explain the notion of gender I use in articulating the claim of gender essentialism, and I begin by drawing a distinction between sex and gender. Although I do not think that there is a bright line distinction between sex and gender, the distinction is useful in explaining the difference between the biological function of reproduction and the socially mediated reproductive function. For convenience I will use "reproduction" to refer to the biological function, and the somewhat archaic term "engendering" to refer to the social function.[3] According to the *Oxford English Dictionary* (*OED*), the roles associated with engendering differ for men and for women; men "beget" and women "conceive and bear." It is a nice semantic coincidence that the activity of engendering in the sense of human reproduction is also a process of engendering in the sense of differentiating women from men according to their reproductive functions.

Next, I explore the nature of social norms, and social normativity because an individual's gender, being a woman or being a man, is a position associated with a social role, a complex set of social norms. I use the phrase "responsive to and evaluable under" to describe the normative pull of social roles rather than the language of obligation, which is more appropriate to describe ethical normativity. To say that an individual is "responsive to" a social norm is to say that the individual's behavior is calibrated in relation to the norm. This calibration does not have to be self-conscious nor does the behavior have to be in accordance with the norm. Both a boy who refuses to play dress-up without thinking about it at all and a citizen who refuses to pay taxes after serious consideration are responsive to

3. "Engender" comes from Latin in + generare; of the male parent "to beget," of the female parent "to conceive, bear." The term is related to "genus" which means "breed" or "race." From the examples in the *OED* the term appears to be used primarily of human reproduction. Its meaning varies depending upon the sex or gender of the individual, which is useful for my purposes.

social norms. The term "responsive to" is intended to cover the full range of possible reactions to a norm on the part of those individuals to whom that norm pertains: from compliance to critique. To say that an individual is "evaluable under" a social norm is to say that the individual is a candidate for evaluation by others in relation to that norm. It is by virtue of being a citizen that an individual is evaluable by others (including institutions like the government) under a set of norms of citizenship (e.g., ought to vote, ought to pay taxes, and so on). The term "evaluable under" describes the status of an individual who, because of his or her social position occupancy, is brought under the umbrella of a set of norms and is thereby a candidate for evaluation by others in relation to those norms.

One central question about social norms is why individuals are responsive to and evaluable under them. What grounds the normative pull of social norms? Why are the Shorts responsive to and evaluable under the patently unfair dining norms of their culture? The view I develop here is that for some social positions individuals are responsive to and evaluable in relation to a social role simply because they occupy the social positions that correspond to the norms. In other words, a Short, just because she is a Short, is responsive to and evaluable under the social norms that articulate appropriate Short dining practices. A parent, just because she is a parent, responds to her culture's parenting norms and is evaluable in relation to them. And, most important, a woman, just because she is a woman, is both responsive to and evaluable in relation to that social role.

But who is to say whether an individual is a Tall or a Short or a man or a woman? Does the individual need to identify with being a Tall or a Short to have that practical identity? Or, alternatively, is social recognition the primary element that determines an individual's social position occupancy? I will argue that for a range of social positions, including gender, social recognition is a necessary element in determining social position occupancy. Social recognition works in a number of ways. In relation to some social positions, like being a citizen, social recognition plays at least three roles in relation to social position occupancy. It plays a causal role when the government's recognition causes an immigrant to become a citizen during a swearing-in ceremony. Social recognition also establishes the definition of the social position: citizenship is granted at birth to persons born in the United States, persons born abroad with at least one U.S. citizen parent, persons granted lawful permanent residence, or persons naturalized. Finally, social recognition determines whether a given individual occupies the social position of citizen and that recognition is embodied in passports, driver's licenses, and other forms of identification. In my discussion of social normativity I focus on the third role of social recognition and the complex ways in which individuals are recognized to be women and to be men. But to establish a connection between gender and social normativity, it is first necessary to explore the distinction between sex and gender.

THE SEX-GENDER DISTINCTION

The sex-gender distinction has been debated and written about extensively by feminist theorists, and I will only provide a sketch of the topic here.[4] Some feminists distinguish sex from gender by basing sex difference on biological criteria and gender difference on social and cultural criteria. "Gender is the social organization of sexual difference" (Scott 1988, p. 2). This distinction between biological criteria and social criteria, or between nature and culture, is probably too sharp and simplistic in itself to be useful. It has received extensive criticism by feminists

---

4. For a helpful discussion of the feminist debate surrounding the sex/gender distinction, see Alcoff (2006, chapter 6) and Mikkola (2008).

who argue that it echoes the dualisms of modern philosophy which are harmful for feminist thinking (Gatens 1996) and that it is implicated in heterosexism (Butler 1990). There are also empirical problems with thinking of sex difference as a biological matter and gender as purely cultural. For one thing, there is good reason to doubt that sex difference is based entirely on biological markers. Human animals are typically divided by sex difference into males and females. The division is based on anatomical, chromosomal, and hormonal criteria. But using these criteria, as feminist historians of biology and medicine have pointed out, we find that there are more than two sexes, even though most individual human animals are either male or female (Dreger 1998, Fausto-Sterling 2000). Pretty clearly, categorization of human animals into just two sexes does not accurately reflect the complexity of what happens naturally or biologically. It is a cultural, medical practice to bifurcate into two categories what is naturally more complex. For this reason, some feminists argue that gender produces sex rather than the other way around.

This is not to deny that there are biological markers associated with being male and female, and with being intersexed, but it is important to recognize the cultural forces involved in categorizing all human animals as either male or female. Still, if we categorize humans using a richer set of sexual categories that do respond to the complexity of nature, then we could say that sexual differences are biological or natural. But if we did, then biological sexual differences would not define just two groups— males and females. And if there are not just two sexes, then there is not a simple projection from biological sex differences to being a man and being a woman.

Thinking of gender as purely cultural also seems simplistic. The reason for this is that part of what it means to be a woman or a man is to be recognized to have a certain kind of body that is linked to certain biological processes like reproduction. And the way that it is linked to those processes is via certain organs, hormones, gametes, and the like. These biological items are linked to the biological processes by virtue of their functions. There is no plausible way of thinking about gender that is entirely detached from bodily, biological existence even if—as we have just seen—those biological processes, or sexual and reproductive functions, are complex and culturally mediated. The bodily aspect of reproductive gender functions provides a limit to the flexibility of the practices that can realize gendered reproductive and sexual roles in a culture. I will refer to the bodily or biological aspects of the reproductive function as its material conditions, which include large gamete/small gamete, gestational environment, and so on. The material conditions of the reproductive function, in turn, are associated with individual bodies that are socially recognized to be either men or women. The fact that gender is realized bodily will play a role in my argument in chapter 3. One reason that gender is not properly attributed to persons is because to be a person does not entail any particular bodily realization or, indeed, any bodily realization of any kind.[5]

I have been discussing why we might doubt that there is a bright line distinction to be drawn between what is natural/biological and what is cultural in relation to the distinction between sex and gender. But my view of gender defined in relation to engendering does not depend upon the truth of the bright line distinction. I am interested in the engendering functions that define women and men. This means that I am interested in those functions as they are realized in human cultures and not as they might occur in nature (leaving to one side doubts about whether that is a live alternative) and not as purely biological functions.

---

5. In contrast, as I explain in chapter 3, social individuals are subject to an indirect embodiment requirement, and so gender is appropriately attributed to them.

There is a very powerful tendency to assume that the social norms that define the engendering function in a given culture correspond closely to the natural norms intrinsic to biological reproductive functioning. This picture, if correct, would provide a nonsocial justification for social roles by appealing to nature and to biology. But there is a vast gulf between the elaborate and diverse social norms governing engendering and its relatively meager set of material conditions or requirements. The social norms governing engendering cannot be "read off" of natural norms or given an adequate biological justification. The gap between social norm and material conditions is simply too large.

To see this, consider the natural phenomenon of feeding. Feeding is an animal function, and it is realized in and by animal bodies. In human societies, feeding (which requires bodies with specific organs—mouths, tongues, stomachs, intestines along with other material conditions) is elaborated into the social function of dining by an array of social norms. Dining is a socially mediated form of feeding. Like the engendering functions I have been discussing, dining is connected intimately to biology and to bodies and their organs. The many, elaborate social norms that govern dining are just like the many, elaborate social norms that govern engendering. Engendering is to reproduction as dining is to feeding.

Let me elaborate on this analogy. Both dining and engendering are constrained by material conditions. If you eat a poisonous berry you will die, and likewise procreation fails unless certain material conditions are met. However, the material conditions that constrain dining do not explain either the elaborate social organization of dining or the immense variety of dining practices. Some dining practices might be directly connected to its material conditions. Perhaps using a particular hand to eat, or bans on certain foods, is related to food hygiene, and the threat of food poisoning. But most of the cultural rules and practices that govern dining cannot be explained by its material conditions. In stressing that the engendering functions that define gender are socially mediated, I do not mean to ignore the fact that they have material conditions. The material conditions that constrain engendering do create some limits on the flexibility and range of activities that can be successful. But aside from a relatively limited number of gender-specific functions (e.g., gestation) and a relatively narrow set of material conditions (e.g., sperm and ovum), there is room for a lot of variation even in the material constraints on engendering practices. Reproductive technologies have altered, at least for some, the material requirements of successful engendering, for example, a normal sperm count or ovulation. So, while it is the case that there are material conditions for engendering, these conditions themselves are not fixed. Indeed, since contemporary social norms governing family formation, and, hence, engendering in a broad sense, include families in which children are not biological offspring of their parents, it is possible to engender without satisfying any of the material constraints that govern biological reproduction.

The slogan "engendering is to reproduction as dining is to feeding" is meant to help us resist the tendency to think that engendering social roles are firmly and tightly connected to the requirements of nature—for example, its material conditions. The analogy is meant to make visible the gulf between social normativity and natural or biological normativity, and in this way to contribute to the "debunking" project characteristic of some social constructivists (Haslanger 2003).

In closing, it is useful to review why feminists find it helpful to distinguish between sex and gender even if there is neither a bright line contrast between biological sex differences and social gender differences nor direct mapping from one to the other. First, thinking about gender as a social or cultural role responds to the variability in specific manifestations of gender around the globe and in different historical periods.[6] It thereby avoids the trap of overgeneralization about women and men that anti-essentialist feminists have articulated (Spelman 1988). More important perhaps, it removes gender from the supposed fixity of nature and the biological world, which, in turn, allows for the possibility of freedom and change.[7] The possible range of gender roles includes as yet unrealized nonpatriarchal forms of engendering.[8] If we thought that the organization and structure of engendering were unjust, there is nothing—in principle—in its material conditions that would block our attempt to change that organization and structure. The material conditions of engendering, just like the material conditions for dining, radically underdetermine their cultural manifestations. Indeed, we could decide to change the material conditions of engendering in pursuit of social justice (Firestone 1970). My definition of gender—being a woman and being a man—ties these social positions to engendering; to be a woman is to be recognized to have a particular function in engendering, to be a man is to be recognized to have a different function in engendering. If human offspring were cloned, and gestated in laboratories, and there was no binary division of engendering functions and associated gender norms, then no individuals would satisfy my definition. In that society there would be no women and no men (according to my definition of those social positions), although there would be female and male human beings.

6. Some argue that biological sex differences in nature have enormous variability in behavior and expression, but I will not pursue that point here (Dupre 1993).
7. I say "supposed fixity" of the biological world because this point presupposes that the biological or natural world itself is not dynamic and full of variation and change.
8. Gay and lesbian families formed through adoption or ART may already be realizing nonpatriarchal forms of engendering although full social recognition is not yet a reality in the United States. The political process of full social recognition for gay and lesbian parents and families is one example of the process towards social justice made possible by changing the material conditions of engendering.

Being a man and being a woman are social positions with bifurcated social norms that cluster around the engendering function. To be a woman is to be recognized as having a body that plays one role in the engendering function; women conceive and bear. To be a man is to be recognized as having a body that plays another role in the engendering function; men beget. The social norms include, but are not limited to, those attaching to different gestational roles and to different parenting roles. Because gestational and parenting roles themselves are manifested in very different ways in different cultures, and in different historical periods, there is no useful way to fill in the blank. The key point is that engendering is a social function with two primary social positions, and the associated social roles are specified in contrast to one another. The actual content of the social roles is variable, just as what counts as a good meal varies widely from culture to culture.

My discussion of gender thus far has focused on women and men, and it is time to address the issue of third genders, which anthropologists argue exist in certain cultures. Examples of third genders are the Hijra in India (Nanda 1990) and transgendered individuals in the United States (Herdt 1994). Anthropologists disagree about whether the Hijra are correctly described as a third gender or should be categorized as male homosexuals. And there is also considerable debate in the transgendered community about how to define itself and its members. I do not intend to add to this taxonomic controversy. Instead, I would like to focus on two issues, which I think are important to distinguish.

The first issue concerns the existence of social positions like being a Hijra or being transgendered, and the second issue is whether these social positions are third genders. My framework of social individuals, social positions, and social roles applies to the Hijra and transgendered individuals in slightly different ways. The Hijras are a socially recognized group with deep connections to religion and to social practices like marriage and prostitution. The Hijras also have a fairly elaborate and explicit social role. Finally, to be a Hijra is to be recognized by others as occupying that social niche. The situation of transgendered individuals in the United States (at this time) is less clear, and the reason is that social recognition of the position is not yet secure. For example, the 2010 Census form did not include a third option for transgendered individuals despite political pressure from the transgendered community.[9] The necessity of social recognition in establishing both the existence of a social position (like being transgendered) and an individual's occupying that social position (e.g., by a psychiatrist or a doctor) underlines the importance of political action to secure the availability of both types of social recognition.

The second issue is whether the Hijra or transgendered individuals constitute a third gender. This question underlines the connection in my work between gender and the engendering function, and perhaps also reveals its limitations. The notion of a third gender is compatible with my approach to gender if the third gender itself is described in relation to women and men as I have defined them. For example, the Hijra are sometimes described as "neither man nor woman" where that phrase is explained (or is partially explained) in relation to the Hijra's inability to play either the woman's role or the man's role in engendering (Nanda 1994, p. 381). Similarly, if what it is to be transgendered is described using the notions of being a man and being a woman, and those notions are themselves understood in relation to the engendering function, then the idea of a third gender is compatible with my approach to defining gender. If transgendered individuals are defined primarily in terms of desire, sexuality, and sexual orientation, however, they would

9. There is also debate within the transgender community over whether transgendered individuals are a third gender.

not count as a third gender in my sense of the term.[10] What my focus on the engendering function rules out is a third gender that is defined with no relation at all to the engendering function.

THE SOCIAL NORMATIVITY OF GENDER

My proposal to define the social positions of being a woman and being a man in terms of their different engendering functions is far from original. This way of thinking about gender has been present in feminist theory at least since Beauvoir (1953). But even though the definition is nothing new, it is important to consider some of its features in more detail. First, social positions are associated with complex sets of social norms or social roles. For example, the social position of being a mother or being a father each has an associated social role, which is a complex web of explicit rules (e.g., legal provisions like child support payments) and implicit practices (e.g., primary maternal responsibility for child care). A basic question concerning social roles is, Why are individuals responsive to and evaluable under social norms? For example, why do mothers feel they should be the primary caregiver for their children and why are mothers who do not provide this care subject to normative evaluation by others? Think of the media criticism of middle class mothers (but not fathers) who work outside the home and put their children into day care. Or think about the "latch-key" children of working class or single mothers, who work in order to support their families.

---

10. For a discussion of transgendering that sees it as challenging "the dominant American gender paradigm with its emphasis on reproduction," see Bolin (1994, p. 447).

What is the source or the ground of the normativity that an individual is responsive to and evaluable under by virtue of occupying a social position? According to one important view, the normative pull originates in the agent's decision to adopt a given practical identity (or, in my terms, to identify with a social position), thereby accepting that her behavior is subject to certain norms or reasons for acting. According to this view, the mother, in identifying herself as a mother, thereby accepts the norms associated with maternity as binding on her and those norms provide her with reasons for acting in one way rather than another. Let us call this the "voluntarist" account of the normativity of social agency.[11] Alternatively, it might be the case that the normativity attaches to the social position occupancy itself and does not require that an individual identify with that social position or practical identity. The social role is normative for an individual if she or he occupies a given social position (or has a particular practical identity) whether or not that individual consciously identifies with or chooses that social position. Let us call this the "ascriptivist" account of social normativity. According to the "ascriptivist," the mother in our example is responsive to maternal norms and evaluable by them just because she is a mother quite independently of whether she identifies with her maternal identity. In saying that the mother is responsive to the maternal norms, I do not mean that all her activities conform to her culture's maternal norms. Indeed, a mother might reject and criticize some or all of them. But the very fact that she needs to reject or criticize the norms demonstrates that she is responsive to them. Rebellion is one way of being responsive to a norm; so is compliance.

Both the voluntarist and the ascriptivist explanations of social normativity seem to capture important elements of a

11. Christine Korsgaard (1996, 2003) is a prominent proponent of the voluntarist approach. I consider her position further in relation to the question of the unity of the agent self in chapter 5.

complex phenomenon. For example, there are clearly social positions, such as being a priest, in which the sincere and explicit identification with the position is part of what brings an individual under the corresponding set of norms. But there are also other social positions, such as being a citizen or being a mother, in which the normativity seems primarily to attach to the social position occupancy itself. Think of a citizen, who refuses to identify as a citizen of an unjust regime. Does her refusal thereby absolve her of the duties of citizenship? Isn't it rather the case that her refusal to obey has its significance just because her actions are evaluable in relation to the norms of citizenship?

Of course, very often these social agents do in fact identify with their respective social positions, but that is not what brings them under its normative umbrella. A mother who does not identify with her maternal role is not thereby freed of its norms; rather, it is because she *is* a mother that she feels the normative pull of that social role and is evaluable by the maternal norms of her culture. These examples suggest that voluntarism, which makes practical identification with a social position a necessary condition of its normative hold on the agent, is not true with regard to all social positions. In some cases the ascriptivist, who makes social position occupancy the necessary feature that grounds social normativity, seems to be correct. This raises the question of what determines social position occupancy in these cases since the ascriptivist cannot appeal to the agent's practical identification with the social position.

For the ascriptivist social position occupancy—being an academic or a mother or a father—is secured by social recognition.[12] In these cases, social recognition is a necessary condition

---

12. It is important to distinguish two questions. First, what grounds the normativity of social roles? Voluntarism and ascriptivism are two answers to this question. Second, what determines social position occupancy? Although I

for social position occupancy. What is social recognition? It is a complex, holistic status comprised of both public institutional recognition and interpersonal acknowledgment. The government through birth certificates, passports, driver's licenses, and so on recognizes gender and other social identities. In the 2010 census everyone is either M or F in the eyes of the U.S. government. Families, friends, and other interpersonal associations (churches, clubs, and the like) are sources of social recognition. In other words, the social recognition of an individual's social position occupancy is accomplished through a complex pattern of individual and group interactions, and legal and political institutions.

The ascriptivist explanation of social normativity seems to fit the social positions of being a woman and being a man better than the voluntarist explanation. First, there is a genetic argument. Our social positions as girls and boys are fixed long before any practical identification is possible. It is fixed ascriptively by the doctor in the hospital, recorded on the birth certificate, and that initial categorization is reiterated over time through institutions like day care and school, books, toys, clothing, and so on. Second, individuals who do not practically identify with their socially ascribed gender are nonetheless responsive to those norms and evaluable under them. In these cases an individual's responsiveness to a gender norm might be to flout it or to flat out reject it. But, as I explained earlier, flouting a norm implies that the norm is in some way or to some degree applicable to oneself. Why bother to flout a norm that is in no way applicable to oneself? In fact, it is not possible to flout a norm that does not apply to oneself. And a tomboyish girl or a gentle boy will find themselves evaluable by others under

---

pose this question in relation to ascriptivism it also arises for voluntarism. And, a voluntarist about normativity might agree with the ascriptivist that social position occupancy always (or frequently) requires social recognition.

stereotypical gender norms whether they identify with them or not. The girl is described as a tomboy regardless of whether she accepts the gender norms that ground that description. It just doesn't matter. Practical identification with the gender norm is not a necessary condition for that individual to be evaluable by others in relation to it. What does matter is that the individual is a girl, that she occupies that social position.

How can the ascriptivist account of gender normativity accommodate criticism of oppressive social norms? If an individual is responsive to and evaluable under social norms by virtue of her social position occupancy, and the latter is determined by social recognition, then there seems to be little room for criticism and the rejection of oppressive social norms. This seems particularly unfortunate in a feminist explanation of the social normativity of gender. Would a woman living under the Taliban really be under the normative umbrella of their oppressive gender norms?[13] Would a woman in the United States really be responsive to and evaluable under our oppressive gender norms? These are important questions. However, they conflate two distinct areas of inquiry about social norms. The area of inquiry on which I have focused concerns the issue of what makes an individual subject to the normative pull of social roles. Ascriptivism and voluntarism provide answers to this question. And I have argued that with regard to some social positions, like gender, ascriptivism is correct. A woman, just because she occupies that social position, is both responsive to and evaluable under the (oppressive) gender norms of her culture. A second, and distinct, area of inquiry concerns the evaluation of social roles, the norms themselves. Are the gender norms of Taliban society or contemporary American culture themselves socially just? Ascriptivism does not address this question. Hence, ascriptivism is compatible with either ethical

---

13. This question was posed to me by Lynne Baker.

or political criticism of existing social norms. The citizen who criticizes the draft on pacifist grounds and the woman who rejects her culture's gender norms concerning appropriate dress and appearance are engaging in a criticism of the social roles themselves from a political or ethical stance. Rather than impede social criticism, ascriptivism adds to the richness of our understanding of the grip of oppressive social norms by explaining why an individual might feel drawn under the normative umbrella of a social role of which she is also at the same time critical.

The ascriptivist account of the social normativity of gender has two features that are important for feminist theory and politics. I will focus on these ideas in the Epilogue but I want to introduce them here. First, by grounding the normativity of gender roles in an individual's social position occupancy, and not in an individual's endorsement of a practical identity, ascriptivism provides a compelling explanation of why women feel the pull of social norms that they reject or criticize on ethical or political grounds, and why they are assessed under those norms whether they endorse them or not. I think that the ascriptivist account of social normativity is a better explanation of the pull of oppressive social norms than those that mention women's limited autonomy or deformed preferences. Second, an ascriptivist explanation of gender suggests that feminist politics should focus on how the social world is normatively structured and criticize those norms that, individually or in concert, are oppressive to women. Feminist politics should focus on changing restrictive social positions and oppressive social norms as well as on changing individual psychologies. For the ascriptivist, feminism is not all about choice. Following Hegel and Marx, I think feminist politics should be directed toward changing social reality rather than on changing the individual social agent and her choices.

CONCLUSION: LOOKING AHEAD

The ascriptivist view of the social normativity of gender is important for my argument for gender essentialism in chapter 4 because there I distinguish between a social agent's principle of normative unity, which is a mega social role that unifies and determines her other social roles, and the social role or practical identity that an individual might identify with or endorse as her own. A social individual's principle of normative unity often is the social role that she identifies with, but it need not be so. My argument will presuppose an ascriptivist view of gender normativity and not a voluntarist account.

Where does my proposed definition of the social positions of being a woman and being a man leave us in relation to gender essentialism? To be a woman is to have one engendering function and to be a man is to have a different engendering function. Recall that my thesis is that gender is essential to social individuals. I have just filled in the understanding of gender that I use in my argument for gender essentialism. And in chapter 1 I explained what I mean by essentialism. But what about the third part of my claim, namely, that gender is essential to social individuals? What are social individuals? And how do they differ from persons and human organisms? And why should the question of gender essentialism be formulated in relation to social individuals rather than persons and human organisms?

Once we have answered those questions we will have gathered together the components necessary to understand what I mean by the claim that gender is essential to social individuals. From chapter 1, we have the kind of gender essentialism I will be arguing for, namely, uniessentialism. From chapter 2, we have an understanding of what I mean by gender, namely, that it refers to the social positions of being a woman and being a man and that these social position occupancies are determined by the engendering functions an individual is recognized to possess. Once I have introduced the notion of a social individual in chapter 3, we will be ready for the argument for gender essentialism in chapter 4.

▼

3

HUMAN ORGANISMS,

SOCIAL INDIVIDUALS, AND PERSONS

MY DAUGHTER ANNA WAS born in Vietnam, and we adopted her when she was nine months old. If Anna had remained with her birth family in Vietnam, her life would have been different in many respects. She would have grown up in a peasant culture in a rural hamlet instead of in a middle-class, nonagrarian American family. But in either scenario, Anna would be the same human organism; she would be the very same member of the human species. But Vietnamese Anna and American Anna would not be the same person, the same psychological individual. Clearly, Vietnamese Anna would have different memories than her American counterpart. Vietnamese Anna would have had different parents and siblings, a different nationality, and different life experiences from American Anna. She would also have had a different set of attitudes and moral dispositions from her American counterpart, since a child's duty to her parents in a Confucian society like Vietnam are more rigorous and exacting than the expectations in contemporary American society.[1] Using the standard psychological criteria for sameness of persons, Vietnamese Anna and American Anna would not be the same person.[2]

1. The PBS *American Experience* documentary "Daughter from Danang" depicts the misunderstanding that can result from culturally different expectations concerning the obligation of a child to a parent (and vice versa).
2. An objection to this point arises in relation to the causal theory of meaning, which imagines an initial baptism (or introducing event) that fixes the reference of a name to an individual, whose different careers and life experiences we can then

The two Annas would also be different social individuals because American Anna occupies a different set of social positions from those available to her Vietnamese counterpart. American Anna is adopted (a social position with manifold implications for her life) and a student of color. Vietnamese Anna would occupy neither of these social positions. She would not be adopted and she would not be a student of color were she living in Vietnam. Indeed, Vietnamese Anna would not be a generic Asian, which is what American Anna is. Instead, Vietnamese Anna would be a member of the Muong minority ethnic group not the Viet or Kin majority, and her ethnic identity would have considerable significance for her social existence. Vietnamese Anna would be a different social individual from American Anna.

I have just illustrated the way in which human organisms, social individuals, and persons differ from one another and can come apart in a life over time. Of course, the three often coincide in an individual's life, which is why it is easy to overlook that they differ essentially from one another. The difference among them is important for my argument because my claim is that gender is uniessential to social individuals (not to human organisms or to persons). Since many philosophers accept that there is an ontological distinction between human organisms

---

trace through possible worlds. So, for example, when we say of American Anna (reference fixed to that individual) that she might have been Vietnamese Anna, we are referring to the very same individual (in two different possible worlds). My question is:, Which individual is the one referred to in the initial baptism that fixes the referent of the term? Is it the organism or the person? If it is the person, and we are referring to American Anna (that person), then it is not clear to me that she might have been Vietnamese Anna (that person). In some versions of the causal theory (Putnam 1991), a type is associated with the initial baptism or introducing event; electricity is a physical magnitude and not, for example, a substance. In these terms, my suggestion is that it is important to be explicit about the type associated with American Anna at the initial baptism. If the type is human organism, then we get one result; American Anna might have been Vietnamese Anna. But if the type is person, then it is not clear to me that American Anna (that person) might have been Vietnamese Anna. The same point applies to social individuals.

and persons, my central task here will be to justify the claim that we ought to make an additional ontological distinction and recognize the existence of social individuals.[3]

The discussion of social individuals brings into focus the field of social ontology, which is (roughly) the study of social structures and social beings. Social reality is dependent upon our agency for its existence. The dependence is both causal (we create and sustain the structures of social reality) and constitutive (we are collectively responsible for the definitions of the institutions, the rules, and the practices that make up social reality in all its variations). In principle, therefore, the particular social structures (including, but not limited, to social positions and social roles) and the particular kinds of social individuals that exist at any given time are, directly or indirectly, amenable to change. This is not to say that social reality is flimsy or chimerical; on the contrary, and especially with regard to patriarchal gender roles, it is remarkably stable and resistant to change. Of course, social individuals are only one kind of social being; there are also artifacts, laws, traditions, languages, and so on.[4]

For my present purposes, I need to explain what a social individual is, and how social individuals differ essentially from both human organisms and persons. I also will explain why the claim of gender essentialism can be coherently formulated only in relation to social individuals and not in relation to human organisms or persons. If I am right about this, feminist theorists have a compelling reason to admit the category of social individual to their ontology since the issue of gender essentialism is central to

---

3. John Locke's discussion in Book II, chapter 27, of the *Essay Concerning Human Understanding* is a classic source for the distinction between a human and a person. See also Baker (2000, pp. 8–9). Olson (1997) argues that we are human animals and not persons.

4. Baker (2007) refers to these objects as "intention-dependent objects" because their existence is dependent upon the existence of persons with propositional attitudes. For an alternative explanation of social reality see Searle (1995).

feminist theory, even though, of course, feminists differ on the question of both the meaning of gender essentialism and its truth.

Let me say initially that by social individuals I mean those individuals who occupy social positions such as a parent, a professor, a contractor, or a refugee. Most (perhaps all) social individuals occupy multiple positions simultaneously; we are all multitaskers! The norms that pertain to a social individual are determined by that individual's social position occupancies. By persons I mean individuals who have a first-person perspective (or self-consciousness) and are characterized by the related property of autonomy.[5] The first-person perspective is the ability to think of oneself as oneself; it is a kind of self-awareness that uniquely characterizes persons (Baker 2007). The connection between the first-person perspective and autonomy is that the first-person perspective is a necessary condition for the possibility of autonomy, which is a kind of inner self-legislation or self-conscious regulation of our desires, decisions, and actions.[6] The ethical obligation of persons is often grounded in their autonomy. By human organisms, I mean individuals who are members of the human species and who realize the human genotype or satisfy whatever other criteria are proposed to define species membership. Human organisms are subject to biological or functional normativity.

Not every member of the human species is a person. For example, a baby is a human organism, but not a person because human babies lack a first-person perspective.[7] Notoriously, a

---

5. I treat having a first-person perspective and having self-consciousness as referring to the same psychological criterion marking personhood. It is the ability to be self-reflective.

6. One standard account of autonomy refers to a person's ability to act from a self-reflective endorsement of his or her own wants, desires, beliefs. and so on (Friedman 2003).

7. Baker (2007) thinks that babies have a "rudimentary first person perspective" which she distinguishes from a robust first-person perspective (p. 11). I'm not

baby is not an autonomous decision maker and hence is not a person by that criterion either. Conversely, there might well be persons who are not members of the human species, like Klingons, angels, or nonhuman primates. If Klingons, angels, or nonhuman primates have a first-person perspective, then they are persons even if they are not human organisms. Furthermore, human organisms and persons are distinct individuals with independent persistence conditions; recall that American Anna and Vietnamese Anna could be the same human organism, but not the same person. Since persons and human organisms have different persistence and identity conditions, they are ontologically distinct individuals.

Social individuals differ from both human organisms and persons because they are defined relationally as social position occupiers. Social individuals exist in relation to the social world and its network of social positions. Being a social individual is a relational status that is fixed by an individual's social position occupancy. Hence, to be a social individual is always essentially to be an occupant of a social position, or to be in relation to a social world. If the social world did not exist, then social individuals would not exist. Social individuals are essentially relational beings and their existence is dependent upon the existence of social reality.[8] In contrast, to be a person is essentially to have a first-person perspective (or self-consciousness),

---

entirely convinced that youngish babies do have a rudimentary first-person perspective, but in any case, it is having a robust first person-perspective, or self-consciousness, that defines persons. Babies might be potential persons, but they are not actual persons.

8. Later I say that most social individuals are agents and specify three conditions for social agency. The first two conditions are not relational (the capacity for intentional behavior and the capacity for goal directed behavior), but the third condition is relational (the capacity for acting from a perspective or standpoint). The third condition connects the idea of social individuals as agents with the idea of social position occupancy since the perspective or standpoint from which the social agent acts is provided by the social position that agent occupies.

56 | THE METAPHYSICS OF GENDER

which refers to an individual's internal psychological condition or state. An individual person could exist independently of social reality because having a first-person perspective does not require the existence of the social world, but a social individual could not exist independently of a set of social positions and roles. Social individuals and persons have different persistence and identity conditions. Hence, social individuals and persons are ontologically distinct individuals.

What is a first-person perspective? It is not enough simply to have a point of view or perspective on the world; it is not enough simply to be selfish. Young children are notoriously self-centered; they are firmly planted in their own perspective on the world. For a first-person perspective, an individual must be aware of herself as someone who can think about herself. "Anything that can wonder how it will die ipso facto has a first-person perspective and thus is a person" (Baker, 2007, p. 10). I'm not sure when the first-person perspective emerges—for my daughter, the realization that she would die happened full force around age twelve. But it is clear that young children occupy social positions like that of toddler, big sister, and grandchild; they are social individuals, without (yet) being persons.

Social individuals and human organisms are also ontologically distinct individuals. Unlike a social individual, a human organism is not dependent upon the existence of a social world for its existence. Recall that American Anna and Vietnamese Anna could be the very same human organism but not the very same social individual because of the very different range of social positions available to them. The two Annas would be different social individuals because to be a social individual is to be essentially related to a particular social world and set of social positions. Since human organisms and social individuals have different persistence and identity conditions, social individuals and human organisms are ontologically distinct individuals.

I have just argued that three types of individuals—humans, social individuals, and persons—differ from one another essentially. In many instances, however, they coincide in our lives; each of us, for example, lives this interesting and complicated ontological coincidence. And in many cases the coincidence persists throughout an individual's life or throughout most of an individual's life. There are also lives like Anna's, where the three kinds of individuals that we are become visible. I call the tripartite ontological complexity of our existence "the trinity." Once we draw these distinctions and realize that we are ontologically complex, however, two important questions emerge. First, how can we understand the relationship among the elements of the trinity? Second, how should we understand the self given the ontological complexity of what we are? I address the metaphysical relationship among the trinity below, and the ontology of the self in chapter 5.

Before embarking on the argument of this chapter, let me briefly connect the distinction among human organisms, social individuals, and persons to feminist discussions of gender essentialism. Feminist discussions of gender essentialism tend to end prematurely because they either pose the issue in terms of human organisms or in terms of persons. Some continental feminists, for example, reject gender essentialism because gender is a social or cultural category, and humans are natural or biological individuals.[9] For these feminists, if some form of essentialism were true, it would pertain to the natural world and not the social world. In short, essentialism equals biologism about gender, which should be rejected.[10] With these feminists I agree that to have a gender is to occupy a social position, but

9. I do not address anti-essentialism as a general philosophical position because that would require another book. For a criticism of the general anti-essentialist arguments of some continental feminists, see Witt (1995).

10. Marilyn Frye (2005) questions the equation drawn by some feminists between essentialism and biologism about gender.

I disagree with the assumption that essentialism could only be true of natural or biological entities. The equation of essentialism with biologism is not only mistaken but it also ends the discussion of gender essentialism prematurely by not considering that socially constituted beings might have essences.

In the liberal tradition, feminists tend to use the notion of a person as their central ethical category.[11] To be a person is to be capable of self-reflection or to be essentially characterized by the first-person perspective. But the capacity for self-reflection is an inner, psychological, or mental property that exists independently of historical and cultural conditions and social relations except insofar as they are causally connected to its development. But gender is a social position and a social role. If persons, like angels, might not have a gender at all, then obviously persons are not essentially gendered. They are not the right kind of individual. My point is not just that gender essentialism turns out to be false in relation to persons. How could it not be, given what the traditional notion of a person is? Rather, my point is that thinking about gender essentialism in relation to persons short-circuits the inquiry by expressing the position in terms that render it incoherent.

If I am right that we cannot coherently express the central claim of gender essentialism in relation to either human organisms or persons, then there is good reason for feminists to look elsewhere for an adequate ontological footing for the claim. My suggestion is that the appropriate category of individuals to express the claim of gender essentialism is the category of social individuals. There is more to say about the centrality of the question of gender essentialism to feminist theory, and the difficulty of formulating the claim coherently in relation to persons and human organisms, but first it is useful to explore the category of social individuals.

---

11. For an important exception, see Nussbaum (1992).

SOCIAL INDIVIDUALS

Social individuals occupy positions in social reality (Lawson 2005). Social positions have norms or social roles associated with them; a social role is what an individual who occupies a given social position is responsive to and evaluable under.[12] I introduced the idea of a social position and a social role in chapter 2 in relation to gender. Being a woman or being a man is a social position, and whether an individual is a woman or a man is determined by which engendering function that individual is recognized by others to have. But there are many, many other social positions, and there is wide variation of social positions across cultures and in different historical periods. Not only do the types of social positions themselves vary from culture to culture but so also do the particular norms or social roles associated with them. This is especially true of cross-cultural and trans-historical social roles like gender. Understanding gender as a social positions allows us to accommodate the widest possible variation in its normative content as I pointed out in chapter 2, and this accommodation responds to some important feminist concerns about exclusion and overgeneralization associated with gender essentialism (Witt 1995).

The definition of social roles is accomplished in many different ways: by institutions like the law and government, by religious and philosophical traditions, by technological innovation, as well as locally by families, tribes, or communities. In addition, cultural imagery found in literature (broadly construed) and art (also broadly construed) encodes, reinforces, and sometimes

12. Social position occupancy is often determined by social recognition so that an individual could occupy a social position even if she did not (for various reasons) fulfill some of the associated set of norms. So, for example, a mother with limited mobility would nonetheless be a mother insofar as she was recognized to occupy that social position. Thanks to Susan Brison, who pointed out the overly agentic connotations of social roles in an earlier version.

alters social roles. It is important to emphasize, in addition, that social roles often incorporate tacit ways of doing things—of dressing, speaking, moving—rather than explicit rules or lists of "ought to dos." But how are all of our social roles organized and unified into a coherent whole? In chapter 4 I argue that a social individual's gender provides the principle of normative unity that organizes, unifies, and determines his or her other social roles. While there is much to be said about the origin, the definition, and the content of social roles, these topics are tangential to my present purpose. The framework I am outlining is simplified, but the simplification is not a distortion in relation to my purposes here. There are individuals and there are the social positions that they occupy and the accompanying social roles that they enact. I will have more to say about social roles later on, but for now let us think about their occupants.

How should we characterize the occupants of social positions? First, most social individuals are agents; they do not simply occupy a social position, but they act in and through it.[13] Agents are individuals who are capable of intentional behavior, are capable of entertaining goals (singly and in groups) and figuring out how to achieve them, and are capable of acting from a standpoint or perspective. Since most social individuals are agents, they are capable of agency in the sense just spelled out; they have intentionality, can engage in means-ends reasoning, and can act from a standpoint or perspective.[14]

Consider for a moment the social position of being a contractor. The occupant of that position is an individual who acts as a contractor (that is his practical identity) and fulfills a set of norms. The activities include making estimates, lining up

13. Not all social positions require agency on the part of the social individuals who occupy them. For example, being an emeritus professor is a social position that does not imply agency on the part of the individual who occupies it.
14. This description of agency is not meant to apply uniquely to social individuals; both persons and human organisms could meet the three conditions.

subcontractors, selecting and buying materials, and supervising various building activities; each of these activities is associated with norms like punctuality and efficiency that contractors are responsive to and evaluable under. The contractor has intentionality and can engage in means-ends reasoning. A contractor works with others to execute a plan. And he engages in all of these activities from a standpoint or perspective that is different from the standpoint of others involved in the building process like painters, plumbers, architects, and tilesetters. Contractors are social individuals. Here is another example: being an academic is a social position. An individual who occupies that position acts as an academic and her agency is enmeshed in a network of norms that comprise the social role of academic. She prepares classes, grades essays, and does research; she serves on committees, attends department meetings, and collaborates with her colleagues. There are both tacit and explicit norms associated with each of these activities. For example, a junior academic is responsive to and evaluable under a tacit norm of deference to tenured members of the department.

I distinguish social individuals from persons because the first-person perspective is an essential property of persons but not of social individuals, who are essentially social position occupiers. In addition, I said that most social individuals are agents, who have intentionality, employ means-ends reasoning, and act from a standpoint or a practical identity. My description of agency includes the requirement that agents act from a standpoint or practical identity. What is the difference between acting from a standpoint or practical identity and acting from a first-person perspective or a self-reflective identification with a standpoint (and the associated goals, feelings, and the like)? First, an agent's ability to act from a practical identity does not require the agent to identify with, reflect upon, or even be aware of that identity. Think of individuals in the United States who are white and whose social agency is informed by that identity;

they are often not aware of themselves as having a race at all. Nonetheless, the social agency of a white North American is thoroughly inflected by being white; this individual acts from a practical identity without self-consciously endorsing it, or even being aware of it. Social individuals are agents who act from a perspective or practical identity without necessarily endorsing it or self-consciously aligning themselves with that identity. Much of our social agency is, as a matter of fact, like this although, as I mentioned in chapter 2, there are certainly social positions whose occupancy conditions include explicit endorsement of the social role. Much of the time, however, we are responsive to and evaluable under a social role simply by virtue of our occupying the relevant social position.

My claim is that the individual, who occupies the social position of being a contractor or being an academic, is a social individual and not a person or a human organism. Let me try to make this claim intuitively plausible with an example. Consider the different meanings and normative implications that the term "mother" has in relation to human organisms, social individuals, and persons. For a human organism, a biological entity, to be a mother is either to be the origin of the large gamete of an offspring or to gestate the fetus or both.[15] The only normative element in the biological notion of maternity concerns the functional adequacy of the large gamete and the success of the gestational process. In contrast, for a social individual to be a mother is for that individual to be recognized by others as occupying the social position of being a mother, and, by virtue of that occupancy, to be placed under the umbrella of a set of maternal norms. Adoptive mothers or individuals who become mothers through assisted reproductive

---

15. The development of ART complicates the notion of the biological mother since the functions of providing the large gamete and gestating the fetus can now be fulfilled by two distinct individuals. In this case there would be two biological mothers.

technology using a donor egg or a surrogate count as mothers if they are recognized by others as occupying that social position. And if an individual is socially recognized as occupying the maternal social position, then that individual is responsive to and evaluable under the maternal social role of her culture (according to the ascriptivist account of social normativity). Now consider persons and the kind of normative requirements that govern the maternal practice of persons and the grounding of those requirements. According to Sara Ruddick, "To be a 'mother' is to take upon oneself the responsibility of child care, making its work a regular and substantial part of one's working life" (Ruddick 1989, p. 17). In other words, a voluntarist account of maternal obligation defines what it is to be a mother in the context of a maternal ethics. Further, for Ruddick it is not necessary that the individual be the source of the large gamete or play a gestational role and also not necessary that the individual be socially recognized to be a mother. It is not even necessary that the individual be a woman. For these reasons we can read Ruddick's account of maternal ethics as appropriate for persons (whose normative obligations require an autonomous decision to undertake maternal duties) but not for social individuals (who are drawn under the normative umbrella of maternity simply by virtue of their social position occupancy secured by the recognition of others) or for human organisms (who are subject to biological normativity). For different reasons, therefore, neither human organisms nor persons are candidates for being those individuals who are essentially social position occupiers and whose normative domains are fixed by their social position occupancy. Since we recognize social positions whose social roles have an ascriptivist grounding, we ought also to admit the ontological category of social individuals. Later in this chapter, I provide a second argument for including a category of social individuals in one's social ontology, which is that the claim of gender essentialism can be coherently formulated only in relation to social individuals.

Thus far I have argued that social individuals are ontologically distinct from both persons and humans. Social individuals are essentially social position occupiers and they are the individuals for whom an ascriptivist account of social normativity is appropriate. Recall that the purpose of drawing these distinctions is to find an appropriate subject for the expression of claims of gender essentialism, and it is to this topic that I now turn.

GENDER ESSENTIALISM AND SOCIAL INDIVIDUALS

The next step is to explain why we should raise the question of gender essentialism in relation to social individuals rather than in relation to human organisms or in relation to persons. My explanation turns on the account of gender and social normativity I proposed in chapter 2. There I said that being a man and being a woman are social positions, and that an individual is a man or a woman depending upon the engendering function the individual is recognized by others to perform. The engendering functions are associated with a rich, complex, and variable set of social norms. The engendering functions are also embodied because there are material conditions associated with engendering and those conditions, in turn, are associated with bodies. And they are relational functions since they are specified in relation to one another and in relation to a particular social and historical context. Because of these features, gender, being a man and being a woman, is appropriately attributed to social individuals and not to human organisms or persons. Let us consider each of these in turn.

The reason that gender is not appropriately attributed to human organisms is that the human organism is a biological entity whose behavior is subject to evaluation only in relation to biological normativity. But engendering is evaluable in terms of social normativity. Recall that social normativity differs from the normativity characteristic of biological functions (e.g., human reproduction) in two ways. First, it is not species based, but flexible and variable across human societies. Second, it is social in the sense that its normativity is rooted in the social recognitions of others. There is a mismatch between the kind of behavior human organisms engage in and the terms by which it would be evaluated if engendering were attributed to human organisms. Hence, if gender is to be essential to any individuals or kinds, it will not be essential to human organisms. So it is a kind of category mistake to pose the question: Is gender essential to human organisms?

We also cannot formulate the question of gender essentialism intelligibly of persons and there are two reasons for this. The first I discussed earlier, which is that persons are essentially those beings capable of self-consciousness or the first-person perspective. And these capacities are intrinsic, psychological properties of persons. But gender is a social position, and to have a gender is to occupy a social position. It is a relational status and not an intrinsic property. Persons, by definition, are not the kind of individuals that could be essentially gendered. Second, the engendering function has material conditions, and individuals are recognized to be women and to be men by others because their bodies are associated with those material conditions. But persons are defined as having a first-person perspective or self-consciousness and without reference to material embodiment.[16] Given this definition of persons, their embodiment is optional. Hence, persons are just not the kind of

---

16. In footnote 19 I discuss the notion of human persons. (Baker 2007) Human persons are constituted by their bodies and so gender might be uniessential to them.

individuals that could be essentially gendered.[17] So, if we are looking for a coherent statement of the claim of gender essentialism (a claim that could be true or could be false) we should not express the claim in terms of persons. It is a kind of category mistake to pose the question: Is gender essential to persons?

Thus far I have introduced the notion of a social individual, distinguished social individuals from persons, and argued that gender essentialism is best expressed in relation to social individuals. Two other candidates, persons and human organisms, were rejected as unsuitable for articulating the claim of gender essentialism. In chapter 4 I will argue that gender is uniessential to social individuals. Before turning to that argument, however, I explain why feminist theorists, in particular, ought to embrace the category of social individuals, and I also address the question of the ontological relationship among human organisms, social individuals and persons.

WHY FEMINIST THEORY NEEDS SOCIAL INDIVIDUALS

Let me begin with one possible drawback of my approach—that I needlessly complicate the ontology of the social world by introducing the notion of the social individual. What is lost or missing in the simpler ontological picture of human organisms and persons? What is gained for feminist theory by introducing the notion of a social individual? Perhaps all we need to express the claims of feminism is a dualistic ontology of human organisms and persons.[18]

17. There is more to say about the issue of embodiment in relation to persons and social individuals, and how the two cases differ. I take up this issue later in this chapter and in chapter 5.
18. In arguing that an ontology of human organisms and persons does not provide a toehold for the coherent expression of gender essentialism, I also aim to reject animalism (Olson 1997).

According to this ontology, humans that meet certain conditions (the first-person perspective) are persons, and as persons they are deserving of moral treatment, and legal and political entitlements. The claims and criticisms of feminism can be articulated as the unfair (discriminatory) treatment of some persons (i.e., women), or as the political and legal inequality of some persons (i.e., women). In relation to the dualistic ontology, the question of gender essentialism would be posed in one of two ways; it would be a question about persons (and their gender) or about human organisms (and their gender).

In the preceding pages I have argued that the question of gender essentialism cannot be coherently formulated either in relation to persons or in relation to human organisms. If an intelligible or coherent formulation of the claim of gender essentialism is important for feminist theory, then this is one reason to find the simpler ontology lacking. I am assuming that gender essentialism is not an incoherent view, although it may turn out to be a false view. Recall from the Preface that most people understand the question of gender essentialism, do not consider it to be an incoherent question, and, indeed, find it easy to answer. And, in fact, I think that many feminists would argue that gender essentialism is a false view and not an incoherent claim. But if the argument of the preceding section is right, it makes no sense to formulate the claim of gender essentialism in relation to persons or in relation to human organisms. And if the question of gender essentialism is not intelligibly raised in relation to persons or in relation to human organisms, we have located one issue that is both important to feminist theory and not coherently stated given the resources of the simpler ontology.[19]

19. Baker's idea of the human person is a particularly compelling version of the simpler ontology (Baker 2007). For Baker, humans constitute persons, and so persons can have bodily properties derivatively. But persons as a primary kind are still characterized as having a first-person perspective as their essential characteristic. And no feature intrinsically connected to the body, like gender, could be essential to persons.

But maybe gender essentialism is conceptually incoherent, and not merely false. Or maybe whether feminist theorists can state the claim of gender essentialism coherently is just not important. In response to the first suggestion, let me point out that feminists who oppose gender essentialism argue that essentialism is false on a number of grounds, and not that the claim is unintelligible or self-refuting. In response to the second point, the centrality of the essentialism/anti-essentialism debate within feminist theory is indisputable, and its significance for a wide range of issues in feminist theory is beyond doubt. So there is good reason to reject the suggestion that the issue of gender essentialism is of little importance for feminist theory. Therefore, it seems that there is at least one important issue in feminist theory that cannot be adequately expressed using the simpler ontology of human organisms and persons. And, since the claim of gender essentialism can be coherently expressed in relation to social individuals, there is reason for feminist theorists to prefer an ontology that includes them to one that does not.

Let me summarize my argument for the claim that our ontology should include the category of social individuals in addition to persons and human organisms.[20] First I argued that human organisms, social individuals, and persons are ontologically different kinds of individuals. Then I made a two-part argument to support the claim that social individuals are social position occupiers (at least for some social positions) rather than persons or human organisms. In the previous section I argued for the inclusion of social individuals in our ontology based on the ascriptive character of social normativity and the idea that a social individual is a relational being who is brought

---

20. Recall that my starting position is an ontology of human organisms and persons and my task in this chapter is to explain why we ought to add a category of social individuals.

under the umbrella of a social role simply by virtue of her occupying the corresponding social position. In this section I made a second argument for the inclusion of social individuals in our ontology; the argument is focused on the theoretical resources needed by feminist theory to express a central issue, namely, gender essentialism. I argued that gender essentialism is a coherent claim only if it is articulated about social individuals and that it is an incoherent claim if stated of human organisms or persons. Hence, feminist theorists have good reason to accept the category of social individuals.

The trinitarian ontology of what we are leaves us with at least two puzzles. First, how are the three individuals related to one another when they occupy the same place? What is the relationship among the human organism, the social individual, and the person when they coincide? A second important question concerns the self and how to understand the self, given the complex ontology of what we are. What notion of the self is presupposed by my theory? I address the first issue here, and the second in chapter 5.

THE CONSTITUTION RELATIONSHIP

My view is that the human organism constitutes both the social individual and the person. The constitution relationship is exemplified by the relationship between a lump of clay and a statue. The lump of clay constitutes the statue but is not identical to it. Lynne Baker has defined constitution, which unites individuals of different kinds, as exemplified by the lump of clay and the statue.[21]

---

21. Although I developed my views independently of hers, Baker's series of articles and books on constitution provide an impressive articulation and defense of the concept.

"The fundamental idea of constitution is this: when a thing of
one primary kind is in certain circumstances, a thing of another
primary kind—a new thing with new causal powers—comes to
exist"

—(BAKER 2007, P. 32).

In this chapter I have argued that a human organism and a
person belong to different primary kinds (to use Baker's terminology). If a human organism comes to be characterized by a
first-person perspective, then a person comes into existence; the
human organism constitutes the person, who essentially has a
first-person perspective. Constitution is a relationship of unity
but not identity: "If a piece of marble constitutes a statue, the
piece of marble does not cease to exist, but (I can only put it
metaphorically) its identity is encompassed or subsumed by the
statue. The constituted thing has ontological priority over its
constituter" (Baker 2007, p. 166). When a human organism
constitutes a person, the organism (the constituter) does not
cease to exist, but the constituted thing is a person, a unified
being, and not two (or more) beings.[22] The organism and the
person share many properties (e.g., physical properties like size
and location) at a time, but their essential properties differ.

Now let us imagine that the statue is also a religious object
of veneration. In this case, we might think that the lump of clay
constitutes both the statue and the religious object. The lump of
clay, the statue, and the religious object all occupy the same
location and share certain properties while belonging to different primary kinds. The existence of both the statue and the religious object depends upon their relations to different social

22. The exact nature of the unity of constituted entities is debated in the
philosophical literature. Rea (1995) and Baker (2007) refer to Aristotle's
doctrine of accidental unities (Matthews 1982) to provide an explanation
for the unity and/or a historical precedence for a notion of unity without
identity.

contexts. A statue exists in relation to an art world, which is the world of museums, connoisseurs, and patronage. The religious icon exists in relation to a religious tradition, a church, a temple, and a text. Similarly, I think that the human organism constitutes the social individual (but is not identical to it). And the human organism also constitutes the person. Persons and social individuals (like statues and religious objects) have different essential properties (and persistence conditions). Persons have the first-person perspective essentially, and this defining characteristic is psychological and internal to the individual; social individuals, in contrast, are essentially social position occupiers. Without the social world, social individuals would not exist, but persons could exist without the social world. In Baker's terminology, persons and social individuals are different primary kinds.

To explore this ontological complexity, let me introduce the idea that the constitution relationship allows for branching. Branching occurs when one object (in this case, the human organism) constitutes two different objects (in this case, the person and the social individual). Branching is a common occurrence—for example, a piece of marble can constitute both a statue and a religious object.[23] Think of "The Pieta" by Michaelangelo, for example, which is both an outstanding piece of Renaissance sculpture/art and an object of religious veneration. The piece of marble constitutes both a work of art and a religious object. In relation to our social world, both the work of art and the religious object exist, but we can easily imagine worlds in which one exists and the other does not. In a world of atheists, only the work of art would exist, and in a world of

---

23. For a discussion of constitution as a "many-many" relationship (with branching), see Wilson (2005). Baker endorses branching in relation to examples like the statue, but it is unclear whether she would do so in relation to the trinity. See Baker 2007b, p. 164."

fanatics only the object of religious veneration would exist. Like all artifacts, these objects have relational essential features or perhaps it is better to say that their existence depends upon the existence of a particular social context. What is the relationship between the work of art and the object of religious veneration in addition to co-location? They share many properties in common like shape, weight, and color because the same thing (the piece of marble) constitutes both of them.

One possible concern with the generous ontology that results from branching is that it might lead to the collapse of the distinction between substantial change (an object coming into existence or going out of existence) and accidental change (an object changing properties). If "The Pieta" were turned sideways and used to block an enemy in wartime, would we have to add a third object, a shield, to the work of art and object of religious veneration? I don't think so. There are at least two ways of blocking the open-ended ontological multiplication. The first is to appeal to pragmatic considerations to limit substantial (primary) kinds, and the second is to limit substantial (primary) kinds to those with causal powers or explanatory significance.[24] The kinds of individuals I am interested in here, namely, persons and social individuals, satisfy both of these criteria. Social individuals are of obvious pragmatic interest to us as the agents of social activity, and they also have significant explanatory significance in relation to a feminist articulation of gender essentialism. Or so I argue in this book.

Persons are defined by the internal property of having a first-person perspective, but social individuals are defined by an external relational property, namely, as being social position occupiers. Like statues and objects of religious veneration social individuals exist only in relation to a social world, but

24. For a very useful discussion of these issues see Wilson (2005).

persons, in principle, could exist independently of a social world. Persons and social individuals are essentially different beings. However, in a given instance, the person and the social individual do share many properties in common (location, physical and biological properties) because the very same human organism constitutes both.

Before ending this discussion let me revisit the issue of embodiment. In the view I have just sketched, the human organism constitutes both the social individual and the person. But I argued earlier in this chapter that the claim of gender essentialism made no sense in relation to beings that might or might not be embodied. Now it seems as if there is no difference between the social individual and the person on this score; neither of them is essentially embodied. However, there is a difference between the two cases. Because social individuals are essentially social position occupiers and as a matter of fact many social positions require embodiment (e.g., contractor, parent), the embodiment of social individuals is also required. The same indirect embodiment requirement does not hold for persons, whose essential characteristic of self-reflection could, in principle, be satisfied without any embodiment requirement at all, direct or indirect.

In the next chapter, I bring together the ideas I have developed in chapters 1 to 3 and I argue that social individuals are uniessentially gendered. We enter into our various social positions as men and as women. One motivation for my argument is the observation that there must be some normative unity among all the many and diverse social positions that we occupy both synchronically and diachronically. I will argue that the social individual's gender provides the principle of normative unity for all of that individual's social roles, and for that reason, gender is uniessential to social individuals.

4

THE ARGUMENT FOR GENDER

ESSENTIALISM

I THINK THAT GENDER is uniessential to social individuals, and in this chapter I will argue for this claim. In the preceding chapters I explained the terms that I use in stating my position. The notion of essentialism I focus upon is uniessentialism, which is the view that its essence unifies a heap of parts into a new individual. For example, the functional essence of a house unifies the parts of the house so that a new individual exists over and above the sum of house parts. I define gender in terms of the different engendering functions of men and women. The engendering functions that define the social positions of being a woman and being a man have associated social roles. A man has one set of norms defining his appropriate engendering activities, which anchor a broader set of gender appropriate norms, and a woman has another set of norms governing her engendering function, and her other social activities. The content of these norms—or social roles—are culturally and historically variable. Finally, a social individual is a social position occupier; one social individual might be a doctor, a parent, and an immigrant at the same time (or, alternatively, over time). Social individuals are agents who are capable of intentional behavior, are capable of entertaining goals (singly and in groups) and figuring out how to achieve them, and who act from a standpoint or perspective.[1] Finally, I argued in chapter 3 that

---

1. Not all social positions imply agency. See chapter 3, fn. 13.

the thesis of gender essentialism is only coherently stated of social individuals, and I noted that a coherent articulation of the position is a prerequisite to considering its truth or falsity. For this reason, feminist theorists, in particular, should be open to including social individuals in their ontology.

It is also worth reviewing the ascriptivist account of social normativity that I introduced in chapter 2, which will help us to distinguish between social normativity and ethical normativity. First, a social role refers to what the occupant of a social position ought to do; an individual is responsive to and evaluable under a set of norms just because that individual occupies a particular social position in a particular culture. It is just because I am a mother that I am subject to maternal norms, and which maternal norms apply to me depends upon my cultural location. For many social roles it is not necessary that the individual identify with the social position she occupies, or reflectively endorse the norms attached to that social position to be placed under its normative umbrella. For social normativity, therefore, it is the assessment by others that establishes or grounds its normative pull rather than the individual's acceptance or endorsement of a norm, which is often thought to ground ethical obligation. Hence, social normativity, while a genuine and important kind of normativity, is different from ethical normativity. As I explained in chapter 3, Sara Ruddick's maternal ethics is an example of an ethical theory of maternal responsibility, which does require that the person decide or choose to be a mother and reflectively endorse maternal norms; the obligation arises from the endorsement. When I use the terms "obligation" or "ought" in this chapter I will be using them to refer to the requirements of social normativity. I will not be making a moral claim or ethically endorsing the social norm; instead I will be describing the normative situation of social individuals in relation to the social roles they enact in a given social context.

Since social individuals are essentially social position occupiers, and since they occupy (or could occupy) multiple social positions at a time and over time, the question of their unity arises. How are the mother, the doctor, and the immigrant unified so that there is just one social individual rather than a bundle of social position occupiers? How ought we to think about the unity of our social lives and activities? It is clear that the kind of unity in question is not the unity of the material parts of a concrete object like an artifact. The parts of many artifacts are arranged and connected physically (glued together or nailed together) so that they can realize their functions. Other artifacts, like the Internet, are unified in other ways. The unity in question can be achieved in many ways but its underlying nature is the same; it is a functional unity. Of course, social position occupiers are not material parts that are unified into a new object in the way that the parts of some artifacts are unified. Rather, social position occupiers are agents who enact social roles, which are sets of norms that shape what it is appropriate for them to do in a given social context. The kind of unity appropriate for social agents concerns how the various social roles an agent is responsive to and evaluable under are unified and integrated with one another so that what results is a normatively unified social individual or agent. The parts in question are social roles, sets of norms; we are looking for a principle (or principles) of normative unity that weaves together and unifies a number of social roles into a single social individual.

The intuition guiding my argument for gender essentialism is that the social roles associated with being a man and being a woman are organizing and unifying roles in the lives of social individuals. This is why when I ask my friends and family whether they would be the same individual if they changed gender, they answer "no, of course not."[2] What they mean is not

2. My case for gender essentialism can accommodate the fact that there are or might be individuals who answer "no" to this question. To put the point generally my argument does not include a premise about how individuals (in general) understand themselves. My favorite deviation from the standard response was a

only that they would enact different gender roles but also that occupying different gender positions would have a global impact on all of their social roles, on how they would go about living their lives. They cannot mean simply that they would have different gender roles because they do not have the same response to the question of whether they would be the same individual if they stopped practicing law and opened a restaurant, or stopped styling hair and joined the Peace Corps. These social role occupancies could cease to exist and yet the social individual (who had occupied these roles) would not also cease to exist. Intuitively, gender roles have a global impact on an individual's other social roles, but many other social positions and their associated roles do not.

Before proceeding I want to emphasize that my argument for gender essentialism does not take as a premise the fact that people tend to think that their gender is central to who they are, or the fact that people tend to think that gender has a global impact on their other social roles. My use of these questions is Socratic. I ask innocent bystanders about what they think about gender in order to introduce the topic of gender essentialism in a cogent fashion that is meaningful to them. But their answers serve not to resolve the issue, as my interlocutors might reasonably expect, but rather to begin the inquiry. The truth of gender uniessentialism would explain why my interlocutors answer the question in the way that they do; but the centrality of gender in most people's self-conception is not a premise of my argument.

Instead, as I just explained, I propose to argue for gender uniessentialism by way of answering a metaphysical question concerning the unity of social individuals. I do this because questions of unity motivate the theory of uniessentialism, and

---

philosopher who said she thought she would be the same individual if she were a hermaphrodite (and not a woman) but not if she were a man. I use the question either to introduce the notion of unification essentialism in contrast to kind essentialism or to explain the topic of this book to nonphilosophers.

this is the meaning of essentialism I use in articulating gender essentialism. There are two parts to the metaphysical question of unity. We can ask about the synchronic unity of the social individual, its unity at a time, and we can ask about its diachronic unity, its unity through time. When I talk about the unity of a social individual, I refer to both its synchronic and its diachronic unity. This point is particularly important for agents who occupy multiple social positions at a time, and whose social role occupancies are usually temporally extended, sometimes undergo development, and often change over time. According to unification essentialism, if the "parts" (i.e., the social roles) of social individuals are normatively unified by gender, then gender is uniessential to social individuals.

I argue in this chapter that a social individual's gender, and in particular the individual's gender norms, provide the principle of normative unity for social agents. I argue that gender has normative priority in relation to other social roles in an individual's social agency. A social role has normative priority in relation to other social roles in two ways. First, a social role has normative priority if it is first in importance, if it is the role whose normative requirements tend to trump the normative requirements of other social roles. Second, a social role has normative priority if it prioritizes—that is, if it defines and organizes—an individual's other social roles. If the doctor, who is also a parent, enters into these social positions as a woman, then the norms she follows in these roles are unified, organized, and defined by her gender. If the social position occupier is a man, then the norms are different; they are unified, organized, and defined by his gender. Gender is a principle of normative unity for an agent because the agent's gender norms have normative priority (in both ways described above) in relation to the other social roles that agent occupies. And if gender is the principle of normative unity for agents or social individuals, then gender is uniessential to social individuals.

The central claim I need to establish is that gender is the principle of normative unity for social individuals. I do this in several steps. First, I explain further what a principle of normative unity is and why social individuals might need one. I develop the idea that a social agent must act under a coherent, unified set of norms, and that a coherent, unified set of norms requires a principle of normative unity. I use Aristotle's discussion of the relationship between a life of virtuous activity and other kinds of lives (and the goods that correspond to them) as a model for the relationship between the social role that serves as a principle of normative unity for an agent, what I call the *mega social role*, and that agent's other social roles. Second, I explain why it is reasonable to think that gender provides a principle of normative unity for social individuals in societies like ours. The third step in my argument is to show that gender norms provide *the* principle of normative unity for agents in human societies. I consider two alternative views: (1) that for some agents in some societies the principle of normative unity is another mega social role, like race, and (2) that the principle of normative unity is variable depending upon the individual's self-understanding. After considering, and rejecting, these alternatives, I conclude that gender is essential to social individuals because gender normatively unifies social role occupiers so that an individual social agent exists. I close with a discussion of the relationship between my thesis that gender is uniessential to social individuals and other conceptions of gender essentialism.

Both the idea that the appropriate kind of unity in relation to agents is normative unity and the idea that an agent must act under norms that are unified and coherent at a time and over time require elaboration. After all, one way to understand the plight of many contemporary Western women is that they are subject to inconsistent social roles so that the idea that social agents require normative unity looks simplistic and mistaken. We might also wonder more generally whether social agents need to be unified at all. Why not think of our social agency as a collection or sum of social roles (mother, academic, and so on) rather than as engaged by a social individual, a normatively unified being? It is to a discussion of these ideas that I now turn.

THE NORMATIVE UNITY OF AGENTS

We can all recognize that our social activity is intricately normative. We ponder what we ought to wear in a given situation, what we ought to say to a certain sort of person. My spouse and I are both philosophers, and we joke that his first question is "What should I talk about on the first day of class?" and my first question is "What should I wear on the first day of class?" The "shoulds" in our questions reflect the fact that we are thinking about social norms, what would be appropriate to the situation. The differences between our "shoulds" reflect gender differences in the social roles or the norms that govern being an academic philosopher. Social norms can generate conflict—someone who is both a woman and a philosopher might recognize that her gendered appearance norms lie in tension with the philosopher's traditional norms, which do not include concern for attire. Notice that it is a condition for the possibility of this kind of normative conflict that the norms in question are binding on a single being. No social individual, no conflict. We can, of course, flout or ignore a social norm, but doing so does not cancel out the fact that we are responsive to that norm (and evaluable by others under it) insofar as we occupy a social position and enact a certain social role. Flouting a social norm (or ignoring it) is one way to respond to it and is entirely different from not being responsive to the norm in question in the first place. I could decide to wear a T-shirt, blue jeans, and sneakers to the first day of class, but it would be an act of defiance (perhaps humorous) rather than a socially appropriate act for a philosophy professor who is an aging heterosexual woman.

The norms or obligations of social position occupiers are sometimes explicit. A doctor should "do no harm." But in many cases both the norms themselves and the process through which we "live up" to them are implicit, habitual, and even unconscious. Sometimes the norms emerge only when they are flouted; when a junior faculty member does not attempt to win over her senior colleagues, when the voice is too loud for a concert hall, when you use the wrong fork at a State Department dinner, and so on. Social norms are complex patterns of behavior and practices that constitute what one ought to do in a situation given one's social position(s) and one's social context. As I explained in chapter 2 these norms are importantly public and shared in that they are established by communities and not by individuals, and they govern members of communities as they occupy social positions within that community. Social norms are "what my people do."

Agents or social individuals occupy multiple positions at a time and over time, and each position brings with it a set of social norms: the doctor ought to do this, the parent ought to do that, and the immigrant ought to do the other. Yet an individual agent requires an integrated or unified set of norms that tacitly or explicitly govern his or her social activity, perhaps prioritizing some normative requirements and minimizing others. The very concept of an agent requires normative unity because otherwise there would exist no single entity but simply a collection or sum of social position occupiers and an associated heap of norms. But why is it important that an agent be an individual? Why not think of an agent as a bundle of social position occupiers? One reason that we might think it is not important to have a normatively unified social individual is that we might try to anchor the unity of our social agency on the normative unity of either the human organism or the person. So it is useful to pause for a moment and to recall why this strategy will not work.

In chapter 3, I argued that social individuals differ essentially from both human organisms and persons. They have different persistence and identity conditions. Social individuals exist essentially in relation to a social world and the positions in it, and they are essentially social position occupiers. In contrast, human organisms and persons occupy social positions only accidentally; they might or they might not. If a human organism constitutes a social individual who is a doctor, the organism is a doctor because the organism constitutes the social individual who is a doctor. If an organism constitutes both a social individual who is a doctor and a person, the person is also a doctor by virtue of being constituted by the same human organism that constitutes the social individual who is a doctor. However, we cannot anchor the unity of an individual's social roles in the unity of the organism or person because, as I argued in chapter 3, the organism and the person are not subject to the appropriate kind of normativity. Social roles are comprised of neither the natural normativity appropriate to the human organism nor the voluntarist ethical normativity appropriate to persons. So, we cannot anchor the normative unity of a social agent in the unity of either a human organism or a person. We are in need of an account of the unity of social individuals.

There is good reason to think that social agents are individuals. First, and most important, social position occupiers have responsibilities in relation to the positions they occupy, and we usually assign responsibility to individuals rather than to collectivities. But if a set of social position occupiers were a just a collection and had no unity, then there would be no reason for a doctor also and simultaneously to be responsive to and evaluable under the parental social role (assuming the doctor is also a parent). Second, the examples of social positions we have been considering assume the existence of individual agents. We have been talking of the agent occupying certain positions with the clear implication that the agent is an individual, who might occupy a number of social positions simultaneously. Third, a social individual requires what we might call normative integrity, a blending together of discrete social roles. We can see this most clearly in the case of conflicting social norms like those of a single mother and a doctor on call when a midnight phone call comes from the hospital. For these social roles to conflict there must be an individual who is bound by both sets simultaneously. If there were no one individual bound by both sets there could be no conflict. In my example of the single mother who is a doctor, the individual is responsive to and evaluable under both sets of norms, but she cannot fulfill both sets. If, as I claim, gender is the principle of normative unity in societies like ours then the resolution of this conflict will reflect the gender norms of that individual. In our example the doctor might refuse to work on call at night and in doing so she would be prioritizing her maternal role and achieving normative integrity. Her maternal role "trumps" her physician's role but that does not rule out the possibility of inner psychological conflict. So if part of the plight of Western women is to be subject to conflicting social norms (as in this example), there must be a being that is subject to both sets of norms. To say as I do that there must be a principle of normative unity for the social individual is not to rule out the experience of conflicting norms but rather to provide a basic conceptual requirement for the experience of inner conflict.[3]

The type of unity in question is normative unity. Normative unity is the primary type of unity that is relevant to agents because agents are social position occupiers, and social roles

---

3. In a recent article in the *New York Times* titled "A Labor Market Punishing to Mothers," David Leonhardt describes the way in which the conflicting norms of maternity and professional social roles generate social inequalities (August 3, 2010).

specify what the occupant of a particular position ought to do. Let's think about social roles as "to do" lists for a moment. Suppose I have three different "to do" lists: one for the garden, one for the family, and one for my job. How do I organize these lists into a coherent plan of action? I could prioritize the lists temporally; garden first, then family, and finally job. The temporal sequencing strategy is not useful for our purposes, however, because we are looking for a principle that can ground the synchronic unity of social roles as well as its diachronic unity. What we might be looking for, then, is a social role that we occupy continuously that helps to determine both what our other social roles are and how they relate to one another both at a time and over time. The idea is that whatever additional social roles we occupy, we do so in a way responsive to the requirements of what I call the *mega social role*, which serves as a principle of normative unity for social individuals or agents. The mega social role is prior to the other social roles occupied by an individual and it also prioritizes them (i.e., it defines and organizes the other roles). It is the principle of normative unity of a social individual.

Let me explain further what a mega social role is and how it organizes our social activity by comparison with Aristotelian ethics. When Aristotle asks what human flourishing is, he considers lives that are centered on different kinds of activities: there are lives of reputation and fame, of money making, of pleasure seeking, of contemplation, and of virtuous activities. These lives are all directed toward goods that are worthy of pursuit, but they pull us in different directions. If we recognize these multiple ways of living with their corresponding goods, how can we order our practical agency? Similarly, being a doctor is a way of living, as is being a mother, and both of these ways of living are normatively infused. How can we order our practical agency if we occupy both social positions and are responsive to and evaluable under both social roles? As we all know, Aristotle argues that the function of a human being is virtuous activity so that our good, which is human flourishing, must lie in that activity. Now, Aristotle's famous metaphor of the target might suggest that he thinks of human flourishing as a consequence of virtuous activity. But Aristotle doesn't think that virtuous activity causes happiness or that happiness is a consequence of virtuous activity. Rather, he thinks that a life of virtuous activity just is a life of human flourishing; virtuous activity is the dominant element in a flourishing human life because it is both prior to, and prioritizes, all of the other activities (and goods). We might say that virtuous activity is the principle of normative unity in Aristotle's ethics in that it organizes and unifies a flourishing human life.[4] The pursuit of pleasure and money making are not excluded from a flourishing human life, but their part in it, and indeed, what counts as appropriate pleasure and money making, are both determined by the dominant element, which is virtuous activity. Pleasures are part of a virtuous life if they are moderate, money making must be compatible with generosity, and so on. In a similar way the mega social role is the dominant normative element in our social lives—not as a discrete part, but as the role that is prior to our other social roles and that prioritizes (defines and organizes) all of them. In the next section I make the case that gender, being a man or being a woman, is a mega social role that provides a principle of normative unity for social individuals in societies like ours.[5]

---

4. Earlier I distinguished social norms from ethical norms. Aristotle's ethics is, of course, an ethical theory so that this comparison might seem to mix apples with oranges. I would distinguish Aristotle's ethical normativity from social normativity in several respects. The most important difference is that Aristotle is concerned with giving an account of appropriate ethical decision making. The point of comparison is that the unifying role of virtuous activity is integrated and expressed in all the other activities of a human life; it is not a discrete element in the life.

5. See my discussion of third genders in chapter 2 for my approach to transgendered individuals.

GENDER IS A PRINCIPLE OF NORMATIVE UNITY FOR SOCIAL INDIVIDUALS

In the previous section, I argued that social individuals need to be unified beings, and I explained why the appropriate kind of unity is normative. What we are looking for is a social role that is prior to an individual's other social roles in that it inflects them in a systematic fashion. I have called this a mega social role. To see how the mega social role works to organize other roles, consider the example of being an academic. An academic performs a series of tasks: lecturer, grader, advisor, collaborator, teacher, writer, and colleague. Each of these functions is normatively inflected by the overarching social role of being an academic. Academic norms of writing differ from the norms of journalism and fiction; an academic lecturer is responsive to different norms (and evaluated by others differently) from those of a motivational speaker or a politician giving a stump speech. The sequencing and significance of the various functions of an academic are ordered by that role as well. For example, the activity of teaching in the life of an academic might be secondary to research whereas teaching might be the central activity for an elementary schoolteacher. In our example, the overarching social role of being an academic is prior to, and prioritizes, all of the "parts" of that social role and thereby unifies them. Now it is unlikely that the academic social role is the mega social role we are looking for because it lacks the requisite temporal duration. If the mega social role is the principle of synchronic and diachronic unity for a social individual, it will exist as long as that individual persists. Hence, the norms associated with blessedly temporary social positions like that of "class clown" or "nerd" are not suitable candidates for being the mega social role.

A second characteristic of the mega social role is that it should plausibly inflect or define a broad range of other social roles. Recall that the house functional property both unifies and organizes the parts into a new individual house and determines the (functional) definitions of the parts. A window has its functional role and definition because it is the part of a house. We would expect the mega social role to determine or inflect the roles that it unifies in an analogous fashion. Being a collector or being a hunter may be a lifelong social role but neither is the mega social role we are looking for because each is relatively isolated from other social roles. An individual might be a collector or a hunter without greatly altering his or her other social roles. Intuitively, we have no inclination to say that someone who gives up hunting is no longer the same social individual.

Gender, being a man and being a woman, are social roles that satisfy both of these characteristics. Gender is almost always a lifelong social position. Transgendered individuals are obvious counterexamples to the claim that gender is a lifelong role, since transgendered individuals are often described as having changed their gender.[6] If that is so, then how can gender be a lifelong social role and a candidate for being the mega social role? Remember that we are considering social individuals in our discussion of social roles. And it is reasonable to think that a change in gender marks the end of one social individual and the beginning of another.[7] From being responsive to one set of gendered social norms and expectations (of appearance, posture, activity, and so on) the transgendered individual becomes responsive to an entirely different set of gendered social norms. Indeed, we can find in the experience of transgendered individuals a moving articulation of the centrality of gender in our lives, and the ways in which it inflects our other social roles (Boylan 2003).

6. For a discussion of transgendered individuals as a third gender, see chapter 2.
7. If gender is uniessential to social individuals then a transgendered individual after transitioning would be a different social individual, but not a different human organism or a different person.

I will argue in a moment that being a woman or a man both unifies normatively and inflects systematically the social roles of the parent and the doctor. If I am right, then gender seems to be an example of mega social role we are looking for. Or, in other words, gender seems to be a strong candidate for being the principle of normative unity of social individuals, and hence uniessential to them. But this argument seems to move too fast. It ignores several alternative approaches to the issue of normative unity. First, aren't there other social roles that also satisfy the requirements of being lifelong and central to an individual's social life? In racialized societies like our own, race in particular seems to meet these criteria for being the mega social role as well as gender does. In a racialized culture, race is usually a lifelong social role and many social roles are racially inflected in a systematic fashion.[8] Indeed, several black feminist theorists have made this argument concerning gender (Collins 2000, Crenshaw 1991). Why not think that—in racialized societies—race is the principle of normative unity for some social individuals, and hence is uniessential to them? Second, one might think an individual's principle of normative unity varies depending upon that individual's self-conception. For some individuals gender might be the principle of normative unity, but for others it might be race or religion. It just depends upon what practical identity that individual embraces. Before addressing these proposals concerning alternative accounts of the normative unity of social agents, I want to explore further how gender works as a—not the—principle of normative unity for social individuals.

Recall that agents occupy social positions in relation to which they enact social roles, which they are responsive to and evaluable under by others. My claim is that the social roles or

---

8. Individuals can occasionally change race (the phenomenon called "passing"), but when they do so it is plausible to think that they have become new social individuals.

norms, which govern a social individual (or social role occupier), are unified by that individual's gender, which is itself a
social role. The mega social role acts as a principle of unity
because it has priority over the other social roles of an individual.
This priority is exhibited in two primary ways. First, the mega
social role is prior in importance in relation to other social roles;
in most situations where there is a possibility of normative
conflict the mega social role's requirements trump the requirements of other social roles. Second, the mega social role prioritizes the other social roles associated with social positions that
an individual occupies in order to unify them into a coherent
whole. One aspect of the prioritizing done by the mega social
role is definitional; the definitions of other social roles are determined or influenced by the mega social role. Let us call this the
definitional priority of the mega social role. A second aspect of
social role unification is the idea that the mega social role—the
gender—of the occupant influences which other social positions that individual might occupy, in what combinations and
in what order. Let us call this organizational priority. Although
definitional priority and organizational priority are distinguish-
able aspects of the unifying function of the mega social role, in
practice and in an individual's life they are intermingled. If, for
example, the social role of parent is defined by the gender of the
occupant of that position, then the definitional priority of
gender entails different responsibilities and norms for women
and for men who are parents. The organizational priority of
gender entails that men and women sequence the parental role
differently and manage its integration with other social roles
differently. In practice, however, the pervasive role of gender in
the definition of a parental task and its sequencing and compat-
ibility with other social roles that the individual might engage
in are deeply intertwined. Think of Barack and Michele Obama,
who are both dedicated parents and highly trained profes-
sionals, but whose social roles as parents differ in the precise set

of activities that define their roles as well as organizationally in terms of the sequencing of parental activities with other social roles. It can be difficult to tease out where the organizational difference begins and the definitional difference ends. In sum, our social roles are systematically inflected by the social roles of gender; the norms that attach to social positions are influenced by the gender of the occupant, and the gender of the occupant also influences which other positions an individual might occupy, and in what combinations and order. Gender is both a synchronic and a diachronic principle of normative unity for social individuals.

What kind of an argument could I make to establish this claim? Since the claim is that gender is a normative principle of unity, it is a claim about the normative structure of an individual's social life and activity. This might look like a factual claim that could be verified by polls, surveys, and the like. However, it is not actually a claim about how every social individual in fact defines and organizes his or her social roles; it is a normative claim about how he or she ought to do so in a given society. The "ought" here is the social normative "ought" and not the full ethical "ought." Recall that Aristotelian ethics makes a normative claim about the organization of parts into a functional whole, and not simply a factual (or descriptive) claim. Our lives ought to be centered on virtuous activity. Similarly, the parts of a house are unified and defined by the house function whether or not the house actually serves that function; the function of the heart is to pump blood whether or not a given heart actually does so. Similarly, it could be that our engendering function has normative priority in relation to the other social roles in a given society even if there are individuals in that society whose social roles are not organized by their engendering function. Hence, there is no simple empirical argument in support of my claim (e.g., a poll or a survey) and no simple empirical refutation of it. What I mean is that my claim would not be disconfirmed by the existence of individuals who either do not prioritize gender in ordering their social roles or do not follow the gender norms of their society fully or well.

What I propose to do is to illustrate the systematic impact of gender on social positions and their associated roles in cultures like ours. In particular, the gendered social roles associated with positions that are defined without reference to gender are a puzzle that invites explanation. I suggest that thinking of gender as a principle of normative unity for social individuals is a good way to explain that systematic impact. This argument leaves open the possibility that there might be other principles of normative unity for social individuals, or multiple principles. My argument here leaves these options open and is meant simply to make plausible the idea that gender is a principle of normative unity in societies like ours. To claim further that gender is *the* principle of normative unity of social individuals requires additional argument, which I provide in the next section.

My strategy is to begin with some easy examples, namely, those social positions that are explicitly gendered, whose norms are directly gendered as a consequence. Next, I consider the interesting cases of social positions that are defined without mention of gender. I point out that even if the social position does not have a gendered definition, in many cases the associated social roles (or norms) are gendered. How should we understand this strange interjection of gendered norms? Where did they come from? I suggest that the idea that gender is a mega social role provides a good explanation of this phenomenon.

A few provisos are in order. First, my argument does not assume that we understand ourselves primarily in relation to gender; it is compatible with social individuals having a primary self-understanding (or identification) in relation to race or religion, or with having multiple practical identities. Second, as I just mentioned, the argument is not intended to rule out other possible candidates for the mega social role, or to rule out multiple candidates for the job. Rather, it is intended to explain why I think that gender is a mega social role, and what I mean when I make this claim.

Let's begin with the easy cases. Many social positions have gender-specific definitions, and as a consequence they have gendered social roles: being a mother or a father, a husband or a wife, son or daughter, midwife, prostitute, or priest. If the social world consisted only of social positions with gender-specific definitions, then (leaving aside for now the question of an alternative principle or principles) it would be fairly easy to establish gender as a mega social role that provides a principle of normative unity for social individuals. In this scenario, every social position that we occupied would have a gender-specific definition and gender-specific norms, and the way in which gender threads through and unifies our social existence would be apparent and uncontroversial. Some societies have, or have had, a fairly strict division of social positions between women and men, and for these societies it is uncontroversial that gender is a principle of normative unity for social individuals. And even in societies with less rigid gender divisions, many social positions are reserved for men and others for women, and their norms reflect this gender segregation. In societies like these, it is easy to agree that gender is a principle of normative unity even though some individuals might choose to flout their societies' norms, or might have a different self-conception.

However, there are also societies like our own in which many social positions do not have gender-specific definitions. For example, a doctor is a qualified practitioner of medicine; a parent is a mother or a father. Even if we don't know much about medicine we might fairly assume that the associated social roles do not include gendered norms since there is no mention of a particular gender in the definition of the social position. Along the same lines we might think that since both men and women occupy these social positions, it would be a puzzle if the associated social norms were gendered. If the social role of being a doctor were a male social role, then how could women doctors successfully perform that role?

At this point it is useful to distinguish several things that might be meant by the claim that a social position has a gendered social role (or set of social norms). First, it is useful to distinguish between bi-gender normativity and mono-gender normativity. Either the social role (like being a parent) is bi-gendered and has one set of norms for men and a different set for women, or the social role is mono-gendered (e.g., being a midwife) and has norms appropriate for either men or women but not both. A social role can be bi-gendered or mono-gendered in two ways. Either the role is simply mono-gendered, like being a midwife, or the role has a mono-gendered resonance, like being a cleric. Let me explain what I mean by a gendered resonance. Today, in some contexts, the social position of cleric is defined in relation to men (in Islam or the Catholic Church) but not in others. In addition, the position of cleric was gendered historically. There is a mono-gendered resonance accruing to it, both because of its history and its current gendered definition in some social contexts.

The distinction between social positions with bi-gender norms (e.g., the social position of parent) and social positions with mono-gender norms (e.g., the social position of midwife) often corresponds to the gender of the social position occupants. Both men and women are parents in roughly equal numbers, which apparently generates the need for two social roles for the position. This is an illustration of the way in which gender inflects the norms governing a social position that is not defined in relation to a single gender. In contrast, women almost exclusively occupy the social position of midwife.[9] The case of

9. Since the 1980s, training for male midwives was legal and available in the UK. There are a very small number of male midwives in the United States.

male midwives is instructive in that their presence in Western cultures is highly controversial, which is often the case when a social position with mono-gender norms is occupied by a small number of individuals of the other gender.

The social position of doctor makes a nice contrast with that of midwife since, although men still outnumber women two to one (in the United States), medicine is a profession that has seen increasing numbers of women practitioners. According to many studies, however, women and men practice medicine in different ways (Martin et al.1988). Women cite the central value of compassion whereas men cite the importance of competence. Women spend more time with patients and communicate differently with them, they choose to work part-time more often, and they tend to favor specializations and jobs that are flexible. They earn less money than men and are less motivated by their earnings than men (Rizzo and Zeckhauser 2007). Their significantly lower earnings than male doctors plausibly reflect their family responsibilities.[10] In sum, studies of women doctors show a different set of norms governing the social position of doctor from those of men. Gender influences the central values associated with the social position of being a doctor, and it also influences sequencing of careers, specializations, and job choice. This is an example of the way in which gender serves as a principle of normative unity for social individuals even in a social position that is occupied by both men and women and is defined without reference to gender. Facts like these are best explained by the idea that a doctor's gender serves as a principle of normative unity for that individual.

10. "Despite similar human capital investments and labor market locations, women married to physicians tend to do family, and men married to physicians tend to do career. The findings challenge a meritocratic view and suggest a closer look at the gendered assumptions of the institutions within which physicians reproduce and labor" (Hinze 2000, p. 1).

We find a similar gendered pattern in academia when we look at data concerning the relationship between professional success and becoming a parent.[11] Just to cite one statistic, "early babies" bestow an advantage to men at the beginning of their academic careers but are a serious detriment to women (Mason and Goulden 2002, 2004). It is reasonable to think that this is a consequence of differing norms of parenthood for men and women. There is also evidence to suggest that the timing and sequencing of the social positions of academic and parent are systematically affected by the gender of the individual (Auriemma and Klein 2010). My explanation for this phenomenon is that the agent's gender provides a principle of normative unity that organizes his or her other social positions at a time. That is the moral of the "early baby" story. The normative unity provided by gender also includes the timing and sequencing of other social positions. That is the moral of the different sequences of parenting and professional attainment in the statistics. In other words, many aspects of the "early baby" study make sense if we think of gender as providing a principle of synchronic and diachronic normative unity for individuals.[12]

I have just discussed two examples of social positions that are defined independently of gender but which have bi-gendered

11. A recent *Washington Post* article, "For Working Mothers in Academia, Tenure Track Is often a Tough Balancing Act" by Daniel de Vise, discussed a research paper by Auriemma and Klein titled "Experiences and Challenges of Women Combining Academic Careers and Motherhood" (AAUP Conference, Washington, D.C., June 10, 2010). The paper contains interviews with academic women discussing the inner normative conflict generated by being a mother and an academic.

12. Another explanatory factor is overt sex discrimination and sexism, but they do not adequately account for the statistical variation and patterns. Indeed, I think that the gender norms associated with parenthood and other social activities are discriminatory, and are sexist, and ought to be changed. And I think that an analysis in terms of social normativity is, or might be, helpful in moving toward political change.

norms. I chose examples of social positions that one might expect to have a set of gender-neutral norms. The fact that they do not have gender-neutral norms requires an explanation, and I have suggested that thinking of gender as a mega social role that inflects and unifies other social roles provides a good explanation. There are many other examples of social positions that are defined without reference to gender but that have gendered norms, both in the United States and elsewhere. Clearly, it would be impossible to discuss all of them. But I hope that I have made the case that thinking of gender as a mega social role helps to explain why many social positions have gendered norms even if they are not defined in relation to gender. And if we think about social positions holistically, as interwoven in an individual's life, then we can see how the gendered norms that inflect and unify many of an individual's social roles will have a ripple effect on most of them. Gender is a mega social role, and it is a principle of normative unity for social individuals. But, is gender *the* mega social role, and is it *the* principle of normative unity for social individuals?

GENDER ESSENTIALISM **AND** RACE ESSENTIALISM **AND** . . .

I have just argued that gender is a principle of normative unity for social individuals. And I have tried to make that claim plausible by illustrating the systematic normative presence of gender even where we might not expect to find it, that is, attached to social positions that are defined without reference to gender. But I want to claim more; I want to claim that gender is *the* principle of normative unity for social individuals, not simply one principle among others. In this regard it is important to notice that the principle of normative unity for social individuals is always calibrated in relation to a particular society and that society's available positions and roles. Although I have argued that it is necessary that a social individual have a principle of normative unity, given that the social positions actually occupied by a particular individual depend upon the social fabric of that individual's culture, it is reasonable to think that there might be alternative mega social roles in different cultures.

In the discussion that follows I focus on racial social positions because they have certain features that make them strong candidates for being mega social roles in racialized cultures like our own. In racialized cultures, racial identity (being white, being black, being bi-racial, etc.) is often a lifelong social position, and our race seems to be central to our lives as social agents. Further, we assign racial categories based on perceived characteristics associated with racial difference, and these characteristics are embodied: skin color, hair texture, facial features, and so on. Racial positions are embedded in hierarchical racist social structures and institutions just as gender is situated within the institutions of patriarchy. Because of similarities like these, some feminist and race theorists have provided parallel definitions of gender and race (Haslanger 2000).

My work is motivated by the opposite intuition. I am interested in the ways in which gender is unlike race, sexual orientation, class, and other social positions that are also embedded within hierarchies of oppression. One striking difference between gender and race is the remarkable universality and stability of gender oppression or patriarchy. Patriarchy is truly a social universal.[13] In contrast, the existence and typology of racial categories varies historically and cross-culturally, and

---

13. Anthropologists and historians debate the claim that patriarchy is universal. Lerner (1986) provides a useful overview of the debate, and she is skeptical of the evidence that is cited to support the existence of matriarchal societies. Lerner describes patriarchy as both a historical (i.e., contingent and variable) social structure and a universal feature of recorded human societies.

racial oppression is not a universal feature of human cultures. It is not even a common feature of human cultures. Philosophers of race debate whether our concept of race was invented in the seventeenth century (Zack 1996, McWhorter 2009) or whether a concept of race existed in ancient Athens (Kametkar 2002, Ward 2002). For these questions to be coherent, it cannot be the case that racial positions are universal or are defined in relation to necessary social functions. In contrast, consider the incoherence of the question of whether women and men existed in ancient Athens or prior to the seventeenth century.[14] Viewed from a cross-cultural and trans-historical perspective, race seems like a weak candidate for the mega social role.

However, it could still be that in a racialized society important social functions—including engendering—are legally or conventionally organized around race. Think about racial miscegenation laws in the United States or in apartheid South Africa, for example. What is important to notice in these examples is that the way in which gender and race inflects these social functions differs. The explicit racial restrictions on who can marry, engage in sex, and engender with whom already assumes the gender of the individuals in question. The racial restrictions are associated legally with the central social functions of marriage and procreation, but the latter are implicitly defined in relation to gender. In a racialized culture, race and racial properties may be associated (legally or by cultural norm) with a central social institution like marriage, but they are not connected by definition with it. Race is not connected to any central and necessary social function by definition in the way that gender is.

Why is this an important consideration? We are considering two lifelong social roles and trying to determine whether

---

14. There are parallel debates concerning the existence of homosexuality prior to the nineteenth century or in ancient Athens (Stein 1999, chapter 4).

one of them might be the mega social role. One reason that favors the view that gender (as a matter of fact) is the mega social role is that engendering is a necessary social function in the sense that it is required for a society to persist. Hence, the social roles that are defined by engendering are connected to the continued existence of the society. It makes some sense that these social roles have priority over other social roles, even roles that are very important in some societies, such as race. The universality of gendered social roles can be understood as a consequence of their definitional relationship to a necessary social function.

I have used the idea that gender is defined in relation to a necessary social function to support the claim that gender is the mega social role even in a racialized society. But doesn't the idea of a necessary social function suggest other candidates for the mega social role—for example, those associated with eating or dining? After all, eating or dining is a necessary social function present in all human societies, and so it would seem to follow that the social positions associated with eating—say, food producer and food consumer—would be candidates for the mega social role. It is likely that every human society has social positions centered on the production and consumption of food, but food production and consumption differs from engendering in important ways. First, the only lifelong social role associated with eating/dining is that of food consumer, but being a food consumer is compatible with also occupying the social position of food producer. So it is unlikely that the social positions that cluster around eating will generate a lifelong social role that could act as a principle of normative unity even within a single society. In contrast, engendering is a necessary social function that reliably generates two distinct lifelong social positions across cultures, and individuals cannot occupy both of them simultaneously. Hence, engendering is a necessary social function that has a feature differentiating it from other necessary social functions in a manner that allows us to see why it might anchor a social individual's mega social role or principle of normative unity.

My view is compatible with the idea that gender norms are racially inflected in racialized societies. In holding that gender is the mega social role I am claiming that it is prior definitionally and organizationally to other social roles, but I am not claiming that gender roles exist in isolation from other important social roles, such as race. For example, as Black feminists have noted, the issue of women in the workplace has an entirely different set of norms for Black women than it does for Caucasian women. And there are many other important differences in the social norms of women of different races in our culture (Spelman 1983, Crenshaw 1991, Alcoff 2006). However, I think that the intersectionality of multiple social roles with gender is compatible with gender being the mega social role.

I have just made the case that gender is a better candidate than race for being the mega social role that serves as an agent's principle of normative unity. It is important to see what I am not claiming. I am not arguing here that racial social positions are not connected to oppression and hierarchy in racialized societies. They surely are. And I am not claiming anything about the levels, kinds, or degrees of oppression associated with race and with gender respectively. Further, I do not claim that it is easy (or even possible) to extricate gender from race in an individual's self-understanding. It is true to say that I enter into social positions as a Caucasian woman and it is likewise true that one characteristic entails social privilege (in my culture) and the other one takes it away in some complex formula. And, as some feminists have stressed, it is probably not possible to unravel these intersecting social positions in an individual's self-understanding. The point I want to emphasize, however, is an important difference between gender and race that has nothing to do with degree of oppression, invisibility of privilege, or the complex intermingling of identities that is each one of us. The important difference lies in the relationship between gender and the fundamental organization of human societies around gendered roles with regard to the engendering function. There are no fundamental social functions organized by race; we can see this by noting that the existence of races is variable; not all societies recognize racial differentiation, and not all of them recognize the same racial categories. My argument that gender is a principle of normative unity for social individuals, supplemented by the claim that gender difference is defined in relation to a necessary social function supports the claim that gender is *the* principle of normative unity for social individuals. This conclusion is conditional, however, since it could be possible that there is (in some human culture) a rival mega social role anchored in a necessary social function. I have argued that race is not that social position, but there could be another candidate. I think as a matter of fact there is no other candidate, but there is no way to show this prior to considering cases.

Let us now consider the idea that an individual's self-understanding determines his or her principle of normative unity. Much of the excellent feminist writing on the topic of personal identity, and on the multiple identities of social individuals (e.g., the theory of intersectionality), focuses on these topics in relation to our self-understanding (Crenshaw 1991). The issue of self-understanding does not play a role in my argument for gender essentialism. Nothing follows directly from my argument concerning how a social individual might understand herself. Indeed, I think it likely that most of us have self-understandings in which our gender is a central element; but many of us might also have other familial, ethnic, racial, religious, or national threads in our self-understandings. In short, the idea that our self-understandings are complex weaves is compatible with my claim that gender is uniessential to social individuals.

Moreover, it is important to distinguish the issue of self-understanding from the question of our ontological constitution as social individuals. Recall from chapter 3 the conditions governing agents: (1) they have intentionality, (2) they can engage in means-ends reasoning, and (3) they are capable of acting from a standpoint or a perspective. Condition (3) does not require a self-reflective endorsement of the agent's principle of normative unity. To be an agent whose principle of normative unity is his or her gender does not require that the agent understand himself or herself in terms of gender, or that the agent self-consciously adopt gender as his or her principle of normative unity. It simply requires that the agent be capable of acting from a gendered perspective or viewpoint.

Let me summarize the line of argument I have been developing. If gender is *the* mega social role or the principle of normative unity for social individuals, then gender is uniessential to them. My argument that gender is *the* principle of normative unity for social individuals has the following components:

1. I argued that agents require a principle of normative unity to organize and unify their social role occupancies.

2. I explained why it is plausible to think that a social individual's gender is a mega social role that is prior to that individual's other social roles and also prioritizes them.

3. To reach my conclusion, however, I needed to rule out other plausible candidates for the mega social role, such as race. I endorse the view that a social individual's principle of normative unity is always relative to a social context, but I argued that gender (as a matter of fact) is that principle in human societies because gender is defined in relation to a necessary social function. I distinguished between a social individual's self-understanding and her principle of normative unity.

Component (3) is necessarily incomplete because it is always open to revision in light of new suggestions of candidates for the mega social role. But I believe I have said enough about the unique features of gender to indicate the kind of response I would make to alternative suggestions. With that proviso in mind, I will conclude that gender is the principle of normative unity for social individuals, and, hence, is uniessential to them.

GENDER ESSENTIALISM REVISITED

It is time to step back and to consider my conclusion. In particular, and given the nature of my argument, the reader might legitimately wonder how gender uniessentialism is related to gender essentialism as the position is normally understood. According to gender uniessentialism, the property essential to social individuals is essential only relative to the actual organization of human societies, which is, of course, contingent. Given the actual organization of human societies, being a man or being a woman is uniessential to social individuals, but there might be societies (including our own in the future) in which the necessary social function of engendering is performed by robots, or by cloning rather than by uniessentially gendered social individuals. This possibility illuminates both the contingent nature of our social organizations and the relational nature of uniessential properties. It is only in relation to the organization of a necessary social function (engendering) in human societies that gender is uniessential to social individuals. But we might think that gender essentialism should be a theory about the intrinsic, nonrelational properties of individuals. And we might also think that the essential properties should not be contingently essential, that is, essential only in relation to a particular social context, which is historical and contingent. Given these differences, it is reasonable to wonder whether uniessentialism even counts as an essentialist theory about gender.

Can relational properties count as essential? Can properties be essential only in relation to a contingent, historical context? The short answer to these questions is "yes." What properties can count as essential and the context within which they are essential depends upon what kind of individual it is. Artifacts, for example, only have essential properties that are relational, and these relational properties are only essential within a social and historical context, which is, of course, contingent. An artifact, like a house, has a relational essence; its functional essence is to provide shelter to humans and animals, and that is a relational property. But this functional property is essential only relative to a contingent social world. We live in houses, but we might not have lived in houses. What is contingent is that there exists a social world with houses; but in relation to the "house" social world, the function of the house is uniessential to it. Similarly, it is contingent that there exists a social world with engendering; but in the "engendering" social world, social individuals are unified by their gender and, hence, uniessentially gendered. In a different social world engendering might be replaced by cloning and in the "cloning" world social individuals would have a different principle of normative unity.

But, would social individuals even exist in the "cloning" world? How could they exist without their uniessential properties? Social individuals would not exist without a principle of normative unity, but they could exist without a particular principle of normative unity. In other words, our unity as agents requires a principle of normative unity, but there could be other social individuals in other worlds with other principles of normative unity. If you think about it, this makes sense. Exactly which principle unifies our agency depends upon the social context, what social positions are available, and how the society is, in fact, organized. If our "cloning" world were no longer organized around engendering, gender would no longer be uniessential to social individuals. But social individuals would continue to exist as long as there was some other principle of normative unity that could thread together, define, and organize a sum of social position occupancies into a social individual.

In my argument for gender essentialism I have tried to do two things simultaneously. I have given full weight to the intuition that our gender is the central thread that connects, organizes, and defines our social existence. But I have also tried to explore this idea in a manner that acknowledges fully the contingency of our social institutions, social structures, and social norms. Viewing gender as uniessential to social individuals accomplishes both of these goals simultaneously, by developing a theory of relational essences that fits within a contingent, historical framework.

5

THE PERSON, THE SOCIAL

INDIVIDUAL, AND THE SELF

I BEGAN WORKING ON the ideas in this book in response to a puzzle about the evident systematic presence of gender in our day-to-day experiences, on the one hand, and the almost uniform rejection of gender essentialism by feminist theorists, on the other. The debates between gender realists and gender nominalists, while both interesting and important, seemed to turn on issues tangential to our day-to-day experiences of gender.[1] I also thought that the omnipresence of gender in our lives primarily reflects a social fact or a complex social structure out there in the world rather than an interior psychological fact about individuals (although of course individual psychologies interact with, and reflect, the social world in which they reside). My initial focus, therefore, was on the social world and its structures rather than on the self that engages with those structures. Since I began with an interest in understanding our day-to-day experiences of gender, it is time to bring the focus back from the social world to the self.

What is a self? Questions about the self, its nature, unity, and persistence, are almost as old as philosophy itself (Martin and Barresi 2003). Is the self defined by internal, intrinsic properties (like psychological or bodily properties) or by external,

---

1. For a recent discussion of important issues in the gender realism/gender nominalism debate, see Frye (2010), Stoljar (2010), Mikkola (2010), and Sveinsdottir (2010).

relational properties (like the self's social situation or its relations to others)? And what (if anything) grounds the unity and the continuity of the self? It would be impossible to address even a small fraction of the philosophical responses to these questions.[2] Instead, I will focus upon three topics, which are central to the views presented in this book. First, I will approach the self from the normative perspective to explore how the ascriptivist account of social normativity applies to the self and how it is related to, and intermingled with, voluntarism. Let us call this the *normative situation of the self*. Second, I will address the ontological problem of how the self is related to the trinity of person, social individual, and human organism. Let us call this the *ontology of the self*. Is the self the person, the social individual, or the human organism? Or is it a fourth entity that is related in some way to the other three? Finally, I will situate my view of the self in relation to recent feminist writing on the topic and, in particular, the view of the self as an embodied and relational being.

The three topics are related to one another in the following way. Begin with the normative situation of the self. On the one hand, the self primarily finds its practical identity through the social positions it occupies and the social roles it enacts; on the other hand, the self is also able to understand itself as avowing or endorsing a particular practical identity or a constellation of identities. Hence, the self is poised between what it is socially determined to be and what it self-reflectively takes itself to be. This distinction corresponds roughly to the difference between the ascriptivist and the voluntarist aspects of social normativity. The normative situation of the self suggests an ontological dilemma concerning what the self is and thus connects the normative perspective on the self to its ontology.

---

2. For a useful discussion of the issues surrounding the self and personal identity, see Schechtman (1996).

The ontological dilemma is as follows: in chapter 3 I distinguished among human organisms, social individuals, and persons, and I explained that the human organism constitutes both the social individual and the person. Given the normative situation of the self there are good reasons to think that the self is the person because the self is capable of self-reflection, of thinking of itself in relation to its practical identity or social roles, and persons are essentially self-reflective beings. But the normative situation of the self also gives us good reason to think of the self as a social individual because its self-reflective activity occurs in relation to the range of social positions or roles available to it. And it is the social individual who is essentially a social role occupier. Hence, the ontological dilemma emerges from the discussion of the ascriptive and voluntarist aspects of the normative situation of the self.

And, finally, both the normativity of the self and its ontology connect to central themes in recent feminist theory about the self. A common point of feminist criticism of traditional views of the self is the concept of the self as an autonomous agent, who is unencumbered by her bodily constraints, her relationships with others, and her social situation. In response, feminists have developed embodied and relational conceptions of the self (Meyers 1997, 2010). In my view the self is embodied because the human organism constitutes both the person and the social individual.[3] Further, the self is a relational being because the process of self-reflection brings the self into relationship with the social individual, who is essentially a social role occupier. Finally, the self is gendered because the self understands itself, forms its practical identity,

---

3. The human organism constitutes both the person and the social individual, and as far as the constitution ontology goes both are equally embodied. However, as I pointed out earlier, given the character of many actual social positions that require the embodiment of their occupants, social individuals must be embodied. This second embodiment requirement does not apply to persons.

in relation to a range of social roles that—as I argued in chapter 3—are unified by gender. Hence, my view of the self is—at minimum—harmonious with recent feminist work on the topic. Indeed, I believe that both the ontology of the self and the normative situation of the self contribute to feminist work on the relational self.

THE NORMATIVE SITUATION OF THE SELF

Only persons—beings who are capable of self-consciousness—are selves, but the process of self-reflection is mediated by our practical identities or social roles. We might understand ourselves to be a mother or a daughter, a politician or a professor, or perhaps all of these together at once. Our practical identities or social roles play an essential part in self-reflection, and they require us to consider the relationship between the self, the person, and the social individual. I explore that ontological issue in the next section. For now let's just focus on the self as a social agent and consider the normative situation of the agent self. What grounds the unity of the self as a social agent? As agents, we must be unified both at a time, because we must act one way or another, and over time, because we are responsible for our past actions. But there are often conflicts among the norms governing the social positions that we occupy. I have argued that what is required is a principle of normative unity that serves to order and organize our practical norms. We stand under multiple (possibly inconsistent) practical norms because we occupy multiple social positions simultaneously and over time. I have argued that gender—being a man, being a woman—is the mega social role that organizes and determines our other social roles.

How is the self as social agent related to its principle of normative unity? If, as I have argued, gender is a social individual's principle of normative unity, how is the self related to it? Must a self understand itself as gendered for gender to serve as her principle of normative unity? Must the self even be aware of her principle of normative unity? In chapter 4 I said that a social individual could be unified by a principle of normative unity without endorsing it or even being conscious of it. The principle of normative unity is practical. It is embodied in a pattern of activity an individual feels obliged to undertake in response to social norms rather than represented to the agent as a principle or rule she ought to follow. More generally in our day-to-day lives we are unreflectively engaged in activities appropriate to the social positions we occupy in a given social context. The unreflective character of much of our social agency is important because it indicates that our agency can be responsive to a norm without our either being aware of the norm or endorsing it. An agent's responsiveness to a norm is one aspect of the way that norms infuse our daily activities. The other aspect is that an individual (or her activity) becomes a candidate for evaluation (by others) under a norm simply by virtue of the social position that individual occupies.

Our social activities are meaningful to us in part because they are responsive to social roles, and because they make us evaluable by others. We live in a normative social world, and the source of the normativity is external to us and does not originate in us. Rather, we find ourselves with a certain practical identity. But, as I mentioned earlier, selves are also self-reflective beings so that the self is often engaged in a process of sifting among various practical identities, embracing some and rejecting others. We are able to stand back and to understand ourselves in relation to a particular constellation of practical identities, endorsing some of them and rejecting or modifying others. How are these two aspects of the self related to one another? How is the unreflective normative activity characteristic of social individuals related to the capacity for self-reflection characteristic of the self?

In a useful discussion Korsgaard explains the practical grounds for our conceiving of ourselves as unified agents:

> "Your conception of yourself as a unified agent is not based on a metaphysical theory, nor on a unity of which you are conscious. Its grounds are practical, and it has two elements. First, there is the raw necessity of eliminating conflict among your various motions....You are a unified person at any given time because you must act, and you have only one body with which to act. The second element of this pragmatic unity is the unity implicit in the *standpoint* from which you deliberate and choose....To identify with such a principle or way of choosing is to be "a law to yourself" and to be unified as such."[4]

The important point in this text is that our understanding of ourselves as unified agents is not theoretical or even conscious; it is implicit and practical. Although Korsgaard says that there are two elements that are the practical grounds for our conception of the self as unified, I think we can distinguish three elements in her account. Let us look at each of them.

The first aspect of our practical unity is a consequence of our embodiment. We are agents who must act, but who, by virtue of occupying multiple social positions, might need to satisfy multiple norms, and these might not all be compatible with one another. Perhaps you ought to attend your daughter's violin recital because you are a mother, and you ought to attend a colloquium because you are an academic. As an embodied agent you can be in only one place at a time; you

---

4. "Personal Identity and the Unity of Agency" by Christine M. Korsgaard, in Martin and Barresi (2003).

can go in only one direction or the other. Our unity is implicit in our embodied agency. But it is only implicit. Because the unity of the agent is a practical requirement of our embodiment, we neither need to be conscious of ourselves as unified, nor do we need to understand the grounds of our unity. I can go to the violin recital without perceiving myself as a unity (indeed, I might feel deeply divided) and without understanding that my action is responsive to maternal norms that organize my social activities. But, however I might understand myself, the very fact of my action necessitates that I am unified.

The second element in Korsgaard's explanation of why our unity as agents is implicit in our activity focuses on the agent's standpoint or perspective. We act from a perspective or standpoint, like that of a mother or an academic. In chapter 3 I said that social individuals were agents who acted from a standpoint or perspective. The standpoint or perspective might be only tacit, however, because we do not need to identify with a perspective (e.g., mother, academic) or even be aware of it in order to act from it. We simply act in response to what is required of us in a situation, and most of the time we do so without representing to ourselves the norms governing our actions, considering them or endorsing them.

The third element of pragmatic unity—that is, identification with a standpoint or identity—is sometimes an element in our practical agency. For example, I might take as a principle for myself never to miss my daughter's recitals, and in doing so I might explicitly identify with being a mother or decide to plan my actions from the maternal standpoint. While much of our social activity occurs without explicit identification with its norms, we do work out practical codes of behavior that turn on our explicit identifications and self-descriptions. This is particularly the case with identities that are deliberately chosen by us upon reflection—like being a feminist or being a vegetarian.

And finally, our explicit practical identity can be forged from many discrete elements.[5]

Korsgaard's description of the pragmatic grounds of our unity as agents provides a useful bridge between the grounds of our unity as agents and our consciousness of that unity. In particular, her account is useful in flagging our embodiment, and our acting from a standpoint as important pragmatic grounds of our unity. As I explained in chapter 3, we are embodied because human organisms constitute social individuals and many actual social positions require embodied occupants. The embodied character of social individuals carries with it an implicit unifying principle; we can move in only one direction or the other because of our embodiment. But embodiment alone does not furnish the principle of unity for social individuals, because they require a normative principle of unity. In chapter 4 I argued that an individual's gender is her principle of normative unity.

The idea of a normative principle of unity connects with Korsgaard's claim that we act from a standpoint or perspective. Social individuals act in and through their social positions, which provide a normative perspective or standpoint for their agency. But, as Korsgaard notes, the agent need not identify with a particular standpoint or perspective when acting from it. Similarly, using my terminology, an agent need not identify with or even explicitly recognize the norms governing a social position she occupies. Of course, as I just mentioned, an agent might on occasion explicitly identify with a normative perspective or standpoint, for example, self-consciously acting as a vegetarian or as a feminist.

---

5. In *The Sources of Normativity*, Korsgaard describes an agent's practical identity in this way: "Practical identity is a complex matter and for the average person there will be a jumble of such conceptions. You are a human being, a woman or a man, an adherent of a certain religion, a member of an ethnic group, a member of a certain profession, someone's lover or friend, and so on" Korsgaard (1996, p. 83).

In contrast to Korsgaard, I distinguish between acting from a standpoint and acting from a standpoint you are aware of, or endorse, or self-consciously identify with. In acting from a standpoint, or from a social position she occupies, an agent is responsive to a set of norms that are associated with that standpoint or social position. The norms are "out there" in social reality, and an individual stands under them just by virtue of that individual acting from a particular standpoint or occupying a particular social position. Moreover, in occupying a particular social position, the agent is evaluable (by others) under the norms that are associated with it. If that agent comes to identify with a standpoint or social position, then the associated norms can become explicit, and the agent can become a self-legislator of those norms. But being responsive to the norms, or evaluable under them, requires neither self-legislation of the norms nor even explicit consciousness of them. Recall from the discussion of ascriptive social normativity in chapter 2 that an individual can be responsive to a social role simply by virtue of her social position occupancy, and she also can be evaluable under those norms by others.

Why does Korsgaard merge (1) acting from a standpoint with (2) being aware of a standpoint and/or identifying with it? One reason is that the visual metaphor of a standpoint or perspective suggests a perceptual orientation toward the world, a vantage point from which to act. Given this perceptual metaphor, it is natural and easy to merge having a perspective with being aware that you have a perspective. The ocular metaphor suggests that (1) and (2) are two stages on a single continuum, the development of a practical identity. But if you begin as I do with the idea of an agent as engaged in purposive social activity rather than as viewing social reality from a perspective, then the transition to an awareness of the social norms being enacted (up to and including acceptance or rejection of them) is neither required nor of a piece with the meaningful activity itself. So, although I have used the metaphors of standpoint and perspective in my explanation of what a social individual is, it is important to keep in mind that they are metaphors and that their connotation of visual perception can be misleading.

Korsgaard also treats (1) and (2) as aspects of one element because genuine normativity enters Korsgaard's analysis only at (2), where an agent identifies with a perspective, forms a practical identity, and makes a "law unto herself" (Korsgaard 1996, Okrent 1999). In chapter 2 I distinguished between ethical normativity and social normativity, which is my topic here. So one way to put the difference between Korsgaard's view and my position is to say that she does not admit any genuine normativity other than ethical normativity. I disagree. I think there is a perfectly good sense in which social normativity is a type of genuine normativity. Consider the example of being a parent. It is just by virtue of occupying that social position that an individual is responsive to and evaluable under a set of parental norms. If the individual is a parent who does not accept the social role associated with that position, the individual is not thereby absolved of his or her parental responsibilities. He or she is blamed. And conversely, an individual who fulfilled the parental role excellently but without ever reflecting about it or making it an explicit aspect of her practical identity would be praised. Surely, a normative framework that finds one parent irresponsible and the other exemplary is a kind of genuine normativity. Only if you thought that in order to stand under a social norm an individual must explicitly understand herself as bound by the norm and/or identify with a perspective would you tend to merge (1) with (2) as two stages on a continuum. Only if you thought that the only genuine kind of normativity is ethical normativity would you conflate the requirements governing ethical normativity with those of social normativity. Most of us most of the time simply are responsive to the norms that govern the social positions we occupy without even being aware of them, much less endorsing them.

I have discussed Korsgaard's account of the practical grounds of the unity of the self to draw upon two deep insights in her view. The first is that selves are unified by the pragmatic requirements of acting, namely, those arising from our embodiment. And the second is that our social activity always flows from a standpoint or perspective. I have added the modification that our activity flows from a practical identity even when, as is often the case, we are not aware of the normative requirements of that perspective but simply responsive to them.

THE ONTOLOGY OF THE SELF

I have been speaking of the self as a social agent, as having a practical identity. This was for the purpose of discussing the normative situation of the self, which is grounded in its practical identities or social position occupancies. This approach to the self might suggest that the self really is the social individual because social individuals are essentially social position occupiers. However, earlier in this chapter I said that the self was a kind of person because persons are essentially capable of self-reflection, and selves also have a capacity for self-reflection. The ontological picture is muddy and it is now time to clean it up.

Let's start with the self, and my characterization of the self as a being that is capable of self-reflection, of understanding itself as a self. If we consider the trinity—human organism, social individual, and person—it would seem that the self would be a person since only persons essentially have a first-person perspective or are essentially capable of self-reflection. However, the discussion of the normative situation of the self established that the activity of self-understanding requires raw materials, and that the raw materials for self-understanding come from the self's social role occupancy. The practical identity of the self, whether explicit, conscious and endorsed, or implicit, practical and habitual, is established by its various social position occupancies. Now it seems as if the self is the social individual. We are faced with an ontological dilemma because there are good reasons to think that the self is the person, but also good reasons to think that the self is the social individual.

One solution to the dilemma might be to claim that a person is a social position occupier, not essentially but accidentally. This seems to be true. In this view the self would be a person, and the person would (accidentally) occupy various social positions. This seems like a solution to the dilemma, and, for lovers of ontological simplicity, it also has the positive outcome of lessening the need for a category of social individuals.[6] If persons can do the ontological and normative work of social individuals, then we have reason to reconsider whether we need to include social individuals in our ontology. However, the proposed solution to the ontological dilemma has a fatal flaw. If a person is only contingently a social position occupier, then it (the person) could exist without occupying any social positions at all; and if that were the case, then the self would have no practical identity to think about or to mull over. A certain and reliable supply of the "raw materials" for the self's practical identity would not be assured. So we need to find another solution for the dilemma.

What we are looking for is a solution that brings the person into relationship with the social individual in a way that ensures that the self is both a being capable of self-reflection and a being

---

6. In chapter 3 I argued that the category of social individuals is needed in order to formulate the claim of gender essentialism coherently, and I noted that the issue of gender essentialism is and has been a central topic in feminist theory. This is an independent reason to think that we need the category of social individuals.

with something to reflect about, namely, a practical identity furnished by its social position occupancies. What I want to suggest is that we consider a basic feature of the ontological relationship of constitution, which is the sharing of properties among the constituters and the constituted beings. Recall from our discussion in chapter 3 that the constituted thing and the constituter can share properties: the statue weights fifty pounds derivatively because the lump of clay weighs fifty pounds. And it is also the case that two objects constituted by the same object can share properties by virtue of that fact. For example, both the statue and the religious object weigh fifty pounds because the clay weighs fifty pounds and the clay constitutes both of them. Further, the statue and the religious object might also both have the property of being venerated, but the religious object has that property directly because of what it is, while the statue in the museum has the property derivatively because it is constituted by the same clay that constitutes the religious object. After all, disputes over the provenance of religious objects that are in museums could arise only if the statue is an object of veneration. But the statue has the property of being an object of religious veneration because the same lump of clay constitutes both it and the religious object. Similarly, the person and the social individual have certain properties because the same human organism constitutes both of them. For example, both the person and the social individual will have a certain height and weight because the same human organism constitutes them both. Now the social individual (unlike the person) is essentially a social position occupier, and if the very same human organism that constitutes a social individual also constitutes a person, the person will be a social position occupier as well—not essentially, like the social individual, but derivatively, because the same organism constitutes them both. Hence, the person will always have a practical identity, indirectly, so long as the very same human organism constitutes both it and a social individual.

The social individual and the person have a different relationship to the practical identity; the social individual is essentially defined by its social position occupancy, but the person is not. So the person has the ability to stand back from the identity or social role, to accept it or to reject it; the person is capable of self-reflection about her practical identities. The person need never think of herself as defined by her practical identities; she may be a mother, an academic, a daughter, but she need not be any one of them. Indeed, as a person, she is not essentially a relational being, a social position occupier. But what the person can stand back from and can be reflective about—her practical identity—is reliably available to the person because social individuals are essentially social position occupiers, and a single human organism constitutes both the social individual and the person.

Given all this, what is the self? The self is a particular kind of person. The self is a person who is constituted by a human organism, where that organism also constitutes a social individual. The self is product of the trinity in the sense that to be a self requires all three elements of the trinity. But the self is not inert, a mere product; rather, the self is actively engaged with its practical identities—enacting them, thinking about them, rejecting them, or avowing them. And it has those practical identities to work with because the very same organism constitutes both the person and the social individual.

Let me sum up this discussion of the ontology of the self and the normative situation of the self by connecting it to recent feminist work on the self. First, let's consider the ontology of the self. The unity of the self is a pragmatic requirement of agency because the human organism constitutes the self, and, in practice, the human organism can only go this way or that way. This is an important theme in relation to feminist theory because it connects our agency (and the unity of the self) to our embodiment. We are embodied selves. Moreover, we are gendered selves. In my view, gender enters the picture not via the constitution of the self (or person) by the human organism; rather, we are gendered selves because the social individual is essentially gendered and the self understands itself via its social roles, namely, in relation to the social individual. Hence, a self is gendered—not essentially but unavoidably—because gender is uniessential to the social individual and because the self understands itself in relation to its social position occupancies.

Second, according to the normative situation of the self, we act from standpoints, which is just to say that we occupy social positions and enact social roles. This point coheres with feminist views of the self as a relational being since the practical identity of the self is realized in relation to the social positions she occupies. Further, the self becomes responsive to and evaluable under a set of norms simply by virtue of occupying a social position. Although the self is capable of understanding itself as a self, and capable of understanding itself as having certain practical identities (and as rejecting others), the capacity for self-reflection does not extricate the self from the ascriptive elements of her normative situation. Moreover a self's *avowed* practical identity, for example, as a philosopher, can come apart from her *ascribed* practical identity, for example, as a wife or mother. These tensions in the normative situation of the self reveal the political dimension of social normativity because they show how ascribed practical identities affect what it is possible for a person to do or to be.

THE SELF IN FEMINIST THEORY

In her original and groundbreaking essay on the self, Susan Brison focuses on the loss of self experienced by trauma victims (Brison 1997). Brison develops a relational theory of the self, which is a view distinctive of feminist thinking about the self, although, as Brison notes, the relational self also has philosophical roots in the Hegel-Marx tradition and in communitarian political philosophy (Brison 1997, p. 12). Brison describes the way in which the experiences of trauma victims both elaborate upon and enrich the kinds of relations that are relevant to recovering (or developing) a self; recovery requires the help of others (e.g., the physical presence of another person), it can be enhanced or secured through loving relationships (e.g., with a child), and it is helped by an audience who can hear and validate a victim's story. Hence, when Brison uses the term "relational" she is primarily referring to connections to other people, whose presence is required for the recovery (or the development) of self.

There are at least two distinct themes in the feminist literature on the relational self. The first theme resonates with Brison's central claim, which is that to develop (or to recover) a self requires relationship with other selves. Brison's claim connects with feminist writing on the self that underlines the significance of other selves in our existence and rejects a view of the self as an isolated, atomistic individual. We are dependent upon others beginning with our parents and ending with those who care for us as we age. Although the position is often described in developmental or causal terms, it is not simply a claim about how we human beings develop. Rather, to be a self is to be in relation to another self; we are all "second persons," to quote Annette Baier.[7] Feminist ethical theories, like maternal ethics (Ruddick 1995) or care ethics (Held 2006), also rest on an ontology of relational selves since both presuppose relationships of care with dependents as their fundamental ethical category.

A second topic in the feminist literature on relational selves concerns relational theories of autonomy. Relational theories of

---

7. "Persons essentially are *second* persons who grow up with other persons" (Baier 1985, p. 84).

autonomy are not unique to feminist philosophy, but feminist theorists have made a major contribution to their development and elaboration. Feminist critics have argued that the traditional notion of autonomy (and with it the traditional notion of a person) is overly individualistic[8] (Mackenzie and Stoljar 2000). As an alternative they have developed a notion of relational autonomy. In this view, autonomy is caused by (or sometimes constituted by) relations with others, which include both the interpersonal relations and the social environment of the agent. Some philosophers develop relational conditions for autonomous agency and others for autonomous action, while yet other philosophers focus on relational conditions for autonomous choice (Holroyd 2010). In a striking example of a failure of a communicative action, Langton (2009) considers a woman who says "no" to a sexual act, intending to prevent the act, but—in her social context—the word both loses its normal effect and does not constitute an act of refusal as it does in other circumstances.[9] The woman is unable to perform the act of refusal by saying "no" given her social context, which is defined by the norms of pornography (Holroyd 2010, p. 104) Notice that there are two relationships in this example; first, between the woman and her sexual partner who does not hear the refusal as a refusal (no uptake), and second between the speech act and its social context. This example of the relational conditions governing autonomous action shifts our attention from relations

8. Feminist social philosophers, who advocate a non-idealizing approach to ethical and political theory, provide another avenue of criticism of the traditional definition of persons as autonomous agents. See Charles Mills, "'Ideal Theory' as Ideology" in DesAutels and Walker (2004).

9. Langton (2009, pp. 47–49), following Austen (1962), distinguishes between the perlocutionary force of an utterance (what it is meant to bring about) and its illocutionary force (what the utterance does). A refusal of sex (i.e., saying "no") can suffer "illocutionary disablement" when its felicity conditions are set by the speech acts of pornography.

with other selves to the social context within which we act. Langton's example suggests that both what one is capable of doing (in this case, with words) and the norms associated with what one is capable of doing are conditioned by the social context within which one acts. According to this theme in feminist work on relational autonomy, autonomous agency is relational in that there are social conditions that make it possible.

As we have just seen, feminist work on the relational self explores both interpersonal relations with other individual selves and also the relationship between selves and their social context in considering the conditions governing autonomous agency. My discussion of the normative situation of the self is an elaboration of the latter theme in feminist work on relational theories of the self. Recall that three factors—acting from a standpoint, being responsive to its norms, and being evaluable under them—ground the normative situation of the self as a social agent. Now consider Langton's woman who cannot perform an act of refusal by saying "no" in a sexual situation. If our sexual reality is defined by pornographic norms, then not only is the woman unable to perform the act of refusal by saying "no," but insofar as she is a woman (i.e., occupies that social position) she will be evaluable under and responsive to these very same pornographic norms according to the normative situation of the self. The woman will be open to evaluation by others (both individuals and institutions) for not understanding that "no" does not enact refusal in a sexual context. For example, the woman might be judged naïve or reckless for thinking that saying "no" might constitute an act of refusal. And she will also be responsive to the pornographic norm governing sexual refusal at least to some degree. For example, a young woman might try to avoid situations in which her "refusal" would be required to stop a sexual act or she might consider perfectly acceptable severe restrictions on her freedom of mobility at night on a college campus. And, of course, these patterns of behavior might be just that—unreflective ways of going about things rather than explicit avowals of value.

Feminists working on the self have also underlined the importance of embodiment in articulating what a self is (Lennon 2010). Since I think that the human organism constitutes both the person and the social individual, the self is embodied in my view. Indeed, as I explained earlier (following Korsgaard), the unity of the self is pragmatically necessary just because of our embodiment. However, embodiment might seem to be too generic a condition to ground a strictly feminist conception of the self; thinking about bodies and embodiment in gender-neutral terms might not be particularly useful for many feminist projects. Indeed, thinking of embodiment in gender-neutral terms might even undercut many feminist theoretical and practical projects by abstracting away the pertinent differences between bodies. This is true, but I want to resist a purely physical account of the gendered self because in the theory I have developed in this book, gender is a social position or category and not a biological or physical category.

But there is another way to understand what it means to say that selves are gendered. Recall that the self understands itself through its practical identities. And its practical identities, the raw materials for its self-reflection, are its social position occupancies, which are essential to the social individual. I have argued in this book that its gender is uniessential to the social individual. And recall that it is by virtue of being constituted by the same human organism that the person and the social individual share certain properties, one of them directly and the other one derivatively. Hence, the self is gendered, not essentially like the social individual, but inevitably. It is possible for the self to step back and reflect upon its gendered practical identities, but it does not thereby extricate itself from them.

In the view I have sketched in this chapter, the self is a certain kind of person, one who is capable of self-reflection, and whose capacity for self-reflection is actually exercised in relation to her social roles. Because these practical identities are essentially gendered, the self is also gendered insofar as she understands herself in relation to them. But even if a self does not consciously understand herself as gendered, the normative situation of the self draws the self under the umbrella of gendered social norms simply by virtue of her social position occupancies. And determining which social positions and social roles are available in a culture, and who occupies which positions, is not up to the individual. I call this cluster of views the *social constitution of the self* and it directs our attention back toward the social world and connects theory to practice or to feminist politics.

EPILOGUE

Gender Essentialism and Feminist Politics

> But the human essence is no abstraction inherent in
> each single individual. In its reality it is the ensemble of
> social relations.
> The philosophers have only interpreted the world, in
> various ways; the point is to change it.
>
> —(KARL MARX, *Theses on Feuerbach, VI & XI*)

FEMINIST PHILOSOPHY IS ALWAYS motivated toward social
change; we seek to understand the social world in order to
change it. In this book, I have tried to understand what it might
mean to say that our gender is essential to us, and I have argued
that on one interpretation of the claim gender essentialism is
true. Given the history of debate over gender essentialism within
feminist theory, however, it is reasonable to wonder how an
essentialist theory of gender *could* be useful in relation to feminist political projects. In fact isn't gender essentialism a position
that precludes or blocks social change? Isn't it the problem and
not the solution? And even if it is not, in itself, a theory implicated in the oppression of women, in what way could it be useful for feminist politics?

Let us consider kind essentialism and its relevance to feminist social change. One of the motivations for the reemer-
gence of gender realism in feminist theory was the need for an
identifiable group as the subject of feminist politics. As I have

emphasized throughout this book, my focus is different. Rather than theorize about women and men as groups or kinds, I was interested in whether an individual's gender is essential to being that individual. Hence, as I explained earlier, several standard feminist criticisms simply do not apply to gender uniessentialism. It does not treat gender as a natural or biological category; it is not inherently exclusionary, and it does not posit an eternal, unchanging feminine essence. But even if gender uniessentialism is not, in itself, an oppressive theory, we might still wonder what use it might have for feminist politics.

By feminist politics I understand advocacy and action in support of political and social change directed toward ending the oppression of women. There are, of course, many important theoretical resources and types of activity that can and do contribute to this project. But gender uniessentialism, the theory described in this book, might seem quite removed from feminist politics so defined. I think that impression is mistaken. Gender uniessentialism directs our attention away from individual psychologies, their conscious and unconscious biases, and "deformed" processes of choice, and toward the social world, its available social roles, and the ways in which its available social roles can and cannot be blended into a coherent practical identity. Moreover, according to gender uniessentialism, our practical identities are essentially gendered. Taken together, these ideas suggest that political and social change for women will require changing existing social roles that (as they overlap, clash, and thread through a life) disadvantage and oppress women.

In saying this I do not mean to dismiss or to criticize important feminist work on deformed preferences (Meyers 1989, Nussbaum 1999) or to minimize the role of gender schemas (Valarian 1999, 2005) or implicit bias (Banarji and Hardin 1996) in perpetuating discrimination against women. This research is of clear importance in helping to document the complex and persistent nature of discrimination against women. Certainly, situational interventions like friendly intergroup interactions and procedural remedies—like anonymous review of applications, journal submissions, and the like—are useful tools for combating implicit bias in some contexts. It is important to note, however, that these approaches focus on individual psychologies and "the moment-by-moment decisions that disadvantage women" (Valarian, 2005, p. 198).

The argument of this book points in another direction, away from a primary focus on individual psychologies, their gender schemas, deformed preferences, and unconscious biases, and toward the social world and its normative structure, which defines the conditions of agency for women. Of course, the two projects I have just described, of documenting and redressing implicit bias with its focus on individual psychologies and the project of examining the social roles available to women with its focus on the gendered social world, can be viewed as complementary pieces of a single endeavor. Indeed, it might be that a substantive change in the psychological workings of individuals would require "culture-wide changes in social organization and practice" because the former are caused by the latter (Hardin & Banarji, in press). But however we want to characterize the relationship between individual psychologies and the social world within which they reside, the argument of this book is that feminist social and political change must include critique of existing, gendered social roles with an eye to changing those that disadvantage and oppress women.

In the view I developed in chapter 5, the self is a certain kind of person, one who is capable of self-reflection and whose capacity for self-reflection is actually exercised in relation to her social roles. Because these practical identities are essentially gendered, a self is also gendered insofar as she understands herself in relation to them. But even if a self does not consciously understand herself as having an essentially gendered practical identity, the normative situation of the self draws the self under the umbrella of gendered social norms simply by virtue of her social position occupancies. And which social positions and social roles are available in a culture and who occupies which positions is not up to the individual to determine. And by this I mean not only the individual who wishes to occupy a certain social position but also those individuals who permit or refuse occupancy.

Consider these stories. According to family lore, in 1946 when she became pregnant with my sister, my mother could not attend graduate school in English because Harvard University did not admit pregnant women.[1] (Women who wanted to do graduate work attended Harvard, and not Radcliffe College, which was an undergraduate college for women.) In this case the social position of graduate student had a definition (explicit or implicit) that precluded my mother's becoming a graduate student while also occupying the maternal social role. This is an example of the way in which the social positions available to women, as they are woven into a life, can clash and diminish possibility. While both maternity and graduate study were available options for my mother in principle, they could not be combined into a single life given the normative parameters of each role. And my mother's gender was her principle of normative unity in that it was prior to, and also prioritizing of, her other social roles.

When my mother-in-law became pregnant in 1939 she quit her job as a bookkeeper not because the position had an implicit or explicit definition that precluded her from becoming a mother, but because the norms governing maternity (at that

---

1. I have not been able to confirm this policy, which may not have been articulated given the small numbers of women applicants. My mother had also recently resigned from the WACS when she married my father and became pregnant with her first child. The WACS did not allow married women to serve.

time and in that place) precluded women from working outside the home. My mother-in-law was responsive to and evaluable under the existing maternal social role just by virtue of being a mother (i.e., occupying that social position) and that social role strongly condemned work outside the home. This is an example of the force of social normativity, which can trump personal interest, financial need, and other motivations.

Finally, when I became pregnant in 1987, the definitions of social positions in academia had shifted from the 1940s to allow pregnant women to be part of the academy, and the maternal social norms had also shifted from the 1930s to find work outside the home acceptable. As we have seen in chapter 4, however, pregnancy and maternity remain uneasy adjuncts to an academic life and place uncertain and inconsistent normative demands upon women academics.[2] And current maternal norms still proscribe practices that make academic work possible for women like the use of day care. Although there has been a shift to allow women into academia and a shift to allow women who are mothers to work, the social roles themselves place incompatible normative requirements on women. As an academic a woman ought to fulfill the duties of that profession but as a mother she ought not use daycare for her children. Since being a woman is uniessential to the social individual, there is no way for that individual to escape or mitigate her situation by combating any psychological bias, gender schema, or deformed preference that she might have. Or rather, doing that will not help her situation. Indeed, even if others in her vicinity took action to combat these psychological or cognitive biases, it would not change the situation. These three examples

2. A recent column in the *Daily Texan* by Jillian Sheridan reported, "When it comes to academia, women still have to choose between family and career. Last week, the *Chronicle of Higher Education* reported that academia is one of the less friendly professions for women with children" ("Academia makes women choose family, career," July 13, 2009).

are intended to illustrate that what needs to change is the social roles themselves, and how they fit and blend with one another (or do not fit and blend with one another) and not only the deformed preferences and implicit biases of individuals.

To the frequently voiced question, "Isn't the point of feminism to give women choices?" my answer is "no, not really." The point of feminism, in my view, is to retool and reconfigure social structures so that they do not oppress and exploit women, and the existing networks of social positions and roles (which vary of course from culture to culture) are a prime example of the social structures that need changing. The landscape within which women choose and act needs to change its normative contours, and then, perhaps, the point of feminism will be adequately captured by the idea of choice.

SELECT BIBLIOGRAPHY

Alcoff, Linda. 2006. *Visible Identities: Race, Gender and the Self.* Oxford: Oxford University Press.

Appiah, Kwame Anthony. 1990. "But Would That Still Be Me? Notes on Gender, `Race,' Ethnicity as Sources of Identity." *Journal of Philosophy* 87, no. 10 (October), 493–99.

Auriemma, Danielle L. and Tovah P. Klein. 2010. "Experiences and Challenges of Women Combining Academic Careers and Motherhood." Presented at the AAUP Conference, Washington, D.C., June 11.

Baier, Annette. 1985. *Postures of the Mind: Essays on Mind and Morals.* Minneapolis: University of Minnesota Press.

Baker, Lynne Rudder. 2000. *Persons and Bodies: A Constitution View.* Cambridge: Cambridge University Press.

———. 2007a. "Persons and Other Things." *Journal of Consciousness Studies* 14, 17–36.

———. 2007b. *The Metaphysics of Everyday Life.* Cambridge: Cambridge University Press.

Banaji, M.R. & Hardin, C. 1996. "Automatic Stereotyping". *Psychological Science,* 7, 136–141.

Battersby, Christine. 1998. *The Phenomenal Woman: Feminist Metaphysics and Patterns of Identity.* New York. Routledge.

Beauvoir, Simone de. 1953. *The Second Sex.* Translated and edited by H. M. Parshley. New York: Alfred A. Knopf.

Bolin, Anne. 1994. "Transcending and Transgendering: Male-to-Female Transsexuals, Dichotomy and Diversity." In *Third Sex, Third Gender: Beyond Sexual Dimorphism in Culture and History,* ed. Gilbert Herdt. New York: Zone, 447–48.

Boylan, Jennifer Finney. 2003. *She's Not There.* New York: Doubleday.

Brison, Susan. 1997. "Outliving Oneself: Trauma, Memory and Personal Identity." In *Feminists Rethink the Self,* ed. Diana Tietjens Meyers. Boulder, Colo.: Westview Press, 12–39.

Butler, Judith. 1990a. *Gender Trouble: Feminism and the Subversion of Identity.* New York: Routledge.

————. 1990b. "Gender Trouble, Feminist Theory and Psychoanalytic Discourse." In *Feminism/Postmodernism*, ed. Linda Nicholson. New York: Routledge, 324–340.

————. 1997. *The Psychic Life of Power: Theories in Subjection.* Stanford, Calif.: Stanford University Press.

Charles, David. 2000. *Aristotle on Meaning and Essence.* Oxford: Oxford University Press.

Collins, Patricia Hill. 2000. *Black Feminist Thought.* New York: Routledge.

Crenshaw, Kimberle. 1991. "Mapping the Margins: Intersectionality, Identity Politics, and Violence against Women of Color." *Stanford Law Review* 43, no. 6, 1241–99.

De Lauretis, Teresa. 1989. "The Essence of the Triangle, or Taking the Risk of Essentialism Seriously: Feminist Theory in Italy, the U.S., and Britain." *Differences: A Journal of Feminist Cultural Studies* 1, 3–37.

DesAutels & Walker. 2004. Moral Psychology: Feminist Ethics and Social Theory. Lanham, Maryland: Rowman and Littlefield.

Dreger, Alice Domurat. 1998. *Hermaphrodites and the Medical Invention of Sex.* Cambridge: Cambridge University Press.

Dupre, John. 1993. *The Disorder of Things: Metaphysical Foundations of the Disunity of Science.* Cambridge, Mass.: Harvard University Press.

Ereshefsky, Marc. 2008. "Species" *The Stanford Encyclopedia of Philosophy* (Fall 2008 Edition), Edward N. Zalta (ed.) forthcoming, http://plato.stanford.edu/archives/fall2008/entries/species/.

Fausto-Sterling, Anne. 2000. *Sexing the Body: Gender Politics and the Construction of Sexuality.* New York: Basic Books.

Fine, Kit. 1994. "Essence and Modality: The Second Philosophical Perspectives Lecture." *Philosophical Perspectives* 8, 1–16.

Firestone, Shulamith. 1970. *The Dialectic of Sex.* New York: William Morrow and Company, Inc.

Friedman, Marilyn. 2003. *Autonomy, Gender, Politics.* Oxford: Oxford University Press.

Frye, Marilyn. 2005. "Categories in Distress." In *Feminist Interventions in Ethics and Politics*, ed. Barbara Andrew, Jean Keller, and Lisa Schwartzman. Lanham, Md.: Rowman and Littlefield, 41–58.

————. 2010. "The Metaphors of Being." In *Feminist Metaphysics: Explorations in the Ontology of Sex, Gender and the Self*, ed. Charlotte Witt. New York: Springer, 85–98.

Fuss, Diana. 1989. *Essentially Speaking: Feminism, Nature, and Difference.* New York: Routledge.

Gatens, Moira. 1991. "A Critique of the Sex/Gender Distinction." In *A Reader in Feminist Knowledge*, ed, Sneja Gunew. New York: Routledge, 139–159.

Gill, Mary Louise. 1989. *Aristotle on Substance: The Paradox of Unity.* Princeton: Princeton University Press.

Hardin, C.D. (in press). "The nature of implicit prejudice; implications for personal and public policy". In E. Shafir (Ed.) *The behavioral foundations of policy.*

Haslanger, Sally. 2000. "Gender and Race: (What) Are They? (What) Do We Want Them to Be?" *Nous* 34, no. 1 (March), 31–55.

————. 2003. "Social Construction: The "Debunking" Project." In *Socializing Metaphysics: The Nature of Social Reality*, ed. Frederick F. Schmitt. Lanham, Md.: Rowman and Littlefield, 301–25.

————. 2008. "Changing the Ideology and Culture of Philosophy: Not by Reason Alone." Presented at the Central APA (April 2007) at a panel sponsored by the APA Committee on the Status of Women.

Held, Virginia. 2006. *The Ethics of Care: Personal, Political, Global.* Oxford: Oxford University Press.

Herdt, Gilbert. 1994. *Third Sex, Third Gender: Beyond Sexual Dimorphism in Culture and History.* New York: Zone.

Hinze, Susan Waldoch. 2000. "Inside Medical Marriages: The Effect of Gender on Income." *Work and Occupations* 27, no. 4, 464–99.

Holroyd, Jules. 2010. "The Metaphysics of Relational Autonomy" In *Feminist Metaphysics: Explorations in the Ontology of Sex, Gender and the Self*, ed. Charlotte Witt. New York: Springer, 99–116.

Kametkar, Rachana. 2002. "Distinction without a Difference? Race and *Genos* in Plato." In *Philosophers on Race: Critical Essays*, ed. Julie Ward and Tommy Lott. Oxford: Blackwell, 1–13.

Korsgaard, Christine M. 2003. "Personal Identity and the Unity of Agency." In Martin and Baressi.

————. 1996. *The Sources of Normativity.* Cambridge: Cambridge University Press.

Kripke, Saul. 1977. "Identity and Necessity." In *Naming, Necessity and Natural Kinds*, ed. Stephen Schwartz. Ithaca: Cornell University Press, 66–101.

———. 1980. *Naming and Necessity*. Cambridge, Mass.: Harvard University Press.

Langton, Rae. 2009. *Sexual Solipsism: Philosophical Essays on Pornography and Objectification*. Oxford: Oxford University Press.

Lennon, Kathleen, "Feminist Perspectives on the Body." *Stanford Encyclopedia of Philosophy* (Fall 2010 Edition), ed. Edward N. Zalta, http://plato.stanford.edu/archives/fall2010/entries/feminist-body/.

Lerner, Gerda. 1986. *The Creation of Patriarchy*. New York: Oxford University Press.

Locke, John. 1924. *An Essay Concerning Human Understanding*. Edited by A. S. Pringle-Pattison. Oxford: Clarendon Press.

Mackenzie, Catriona and Natalie Stoljar. 2000. *Relational Autonomy: Feminist Perspectives on Agency and the Social Self*. Oxford: Oxford University Press.

Mallon, Ron. 2003. "Social Roles, Social Construction and Stability." In *Socializing Metaphysics*, ed. Frederick Schmitt. Lanham, Md.: Rowman and Littlefield, 327–54.

Martin, Raymond and John Baressi. 2003. *Personal Identity*. Oxford: Blackwell.

Martin, Steven C., Robert M. Arnold, and Ruth M. Parker. 1988. "Gender and Medical Socialization." *Journal of Health and Social Behavior* 29 (December), 333–43.

Matthews, Gary. 1982. "Accidental Unities". In *Language and Logos* ed. by M. Schofield and M. Nussbaum. Cambridge: Cambridge University Press, 223–240.

Mason, Mary Ann and Marc Goulden. 2004. "Marriage and Baby Blues: Re-defining Gender Equity in the Academy." *Annals of the American Academy of Political and Social Science* 596, 86–103.

———. 2002. "Do Babies Matter? The Effects of Family Formation on the Lifelong Careers of Academic Men and Women." *Academe* 88, 21–27, *http://www.aaup.org/publications/Academe/2002/02nd/02ndmas.htm.*

McWhorter, Ladelle. 2009. *Racism and Sexual Oppression in Anglo-America: A Genealogy*. Bloomington, Ind. Indiana University Press.

Meyers, Diana. 1989. *Self, Society, and Personal Choice*. New York: Columbia University Press.

―――. 1997. *Feminists Rethink the Self*. Boulder, Colo.: Westview Press.

―――. 2002. *Gender in the Mirror: Cultural Imagery and Women's Agency*. Oxford: Oxford University Press.

―――. 2010. "Feminist Perspectives on the Self." *The Stanford Encyclopedia of Philosophy* (Spring 2010 Edition), ed. Edward N. Zalta, http://plato.stanford.edu/archives/spr2010/entries/feminism-self/.

Mikkola, Mari. 2006. "Elizabeth Spelman, Gender Realism and Women." *Hypatia* 21, no. 4 (Fall), 77–96.

―――. "Feminist Perspectives on Sex and Gender." *The Stanford Encyclopedia of Philosophy* (Fall 2008 Edition), ed. Edward N. Zalta, http://plato.stanford.edu/archives/fall2008/entries/feminism-gender/.

―――. 2010. "Ontological Commitments, Sex and Gender." In *Feminist Metaphysics: Explorations in the Ontology of Sex, Gender and the Self*, ed. Charlotte Witt. New York: Springer, 67–84.

Mills, Charles. 2004. "'Ideal Theory' as Ideology" in DesAutels and Walker (2004), 163–181.

Nanda, Serena. 1990. *Neither Man nor Woman: The Hijras of India*. Belmont. Calif.: Wadsworth.

―――. "Hijras: An Alternative Sex and Gender Role in India." In *Third Sex, Third Gender: Beyond Sexual Dimorphism in Culture and History*, ed. Gilbert Herdt. New York: Zone, 373–418.

Nussbaum, Martha C. 1992. "Human Functioning and Social Justice: In Defense of Aristotelian Essentialism." *Political Theory* 20, no. 2, 202–46.

Olson, Peter. 1997. *The Human Animal: Personal Identity without Psychology*. New York: Oxford University Press.

Putnam, Hilary. 1991. "Explanation and Reference." In *Readings in the Philosophy of Science*, ed. Richard Boyd, Philip Gasper, and J. D. Trout. Cambridge, Mass.: MIT Press, 171–86.

Rea, Michael. 1998. "Sameness without Identity: An Aristotelian Solution to the Problem of Material Constitution." In *Ratio* 11, no. 3 (December), 316–28.

―――. 2000. "Constitution and Kind Membership." *Philosophical Studies* 97, 167–93.

Rhode, Deborah. 1997. *Speaking of Sex*. Cambridge: Harvard University Press.

Rizzo, John A. and Richard J. Zeckhauser. 2007. "Pushing Incomes to Reference Points: Why Do Male Doctors Earn More?" *Journal of Economic Behavior and Organization* 63, no. 3, 514–36.

Ruddick, Sara. 1989. *Maternal Thinking: Toward a Politics of Peace*. Boston: Beacon Press.

Schechtman, Marya. 1996. *The Constitution of Selves*. Ithaca: Cornell University Press.

Schmitt, Frederick. 2003. *Socializing Metaphysics*. Lanham, Md.: Rowman and Littlefield.

Schwartz, Stephen. 1977. *Naming, Necessity and Natural Kinds*. Ithaca: Cornell University Press.

Scott, Joan Wallach. 1988. *Gender and the Politics of History*. New York: Columbia University Press.

Searle, John. 1995. *The Construction of Social Reality*. New York: Free Press.

Sober, Elliot. 1980. "Evolution, Population Thinking and Essentialism." *Philosophy of Science* 47, 350–83.

Spelman, Elizabeth. 1988. *Inessential Woman: Problems of Exclusion in Feminist Thought*. Boston: Beacon Press.

Stein, Edward. 1999. *The Mismeasure of Desire: The Science, Theory and Ethics of Sexual Orientation*. Oxford: Oxford University Press.

Stoljar, Natalie. 1995. "Essence, Identity and the Concept of Woman." *Philosophical Topics* 23, no. 2, 261–29

———. 2010. "Different Women: Gender and the Realism/ Nominalism Debate." In *Feminist Metaphysics: Explorations in the Ontology of Sex, Gender and the Self*, ed. Charlotte Witt. New York: Springer, 27–46.

Sveinsdóttir, Ásta Kristjana. 2010. "The Metaphysics of Sex and Gender." In *Feminist Metaphysics: Explorations in the Ontology of Sex, Gender and the Self*, ed. Charlotte Witt. New York: Springer, 47–66.

Valian, Virginia. 2005. "Beyond gender schemas: Inproving the advancement of women in academia". *Hypatia* 20, 198–213.

———. 1999. *Why So Slow?* Boston: MIT Press.

Ward, Julie. 2002. "*Ethnos* in the *Politics.*" In *Philosophers on Race: Critical Essays*, ed. Julie Ward and Tommy Lott. Oxford: Blackwell, 14–38.

Ward, Julie and Tommy Lott. 2002. *Philosophers on Race: Critical Essays.* Oxford: Blackwell.

Wilson, Robert A. 2005. "Persons, Social Agency and Constitution". In *Social Philosophy and Policy* 22 (Summer 2005), 49–69.

Witt, Charlotte. 1995. "Anti-Essentialism in Feminist Theory." *Philosophical Topics: Feminist Perspectives on Language, Knowledge and Reality* 23, no. 2, 321–44.

———, ed. 2010. *Feminist Metaphysics: Explorations in the Ontology of Sex, Gender and the Self.* New York: Springer.

Zack, Naomi. 2005. *Inclusive Feminism: A Third Wave Theory of Women's Commonality.* Lanham, Md.: Rowman and Littlefield.

———. 1997. *RACE/SEX: Their Sameness, Difference and Interplay.* New York: Routledge.

INDEX

Embodiment
  agency, 113
  gender essentialism issue
    of, 73, 98
  gender-neutral terms
    of, 125
  persons and social
    individuals, 73, 109n3
  self, 109, 109n3, 120–21
  unity as consequence
    of, 112–13
Engendering functions
  food production necessity
    compared to, 100
  as necessary to society, 100,
    101–2
  race and, 102
  as relational property, 18
  reproduction and, 37–38
  sex-gender distinction
    and, 37–40
  social roles and, 42, 100
  terminology, 32, 32n3
*Essay Concerning Human
  Understanding*
  (Locke), 53n3
Essences
  functional, 14, 19, 75, 105
  nominal, 5, 5n3, 24–26
Essentialism. *See also* Gender
  essentialism; Kind
  essentialism;
  Uniessentialism;
  Individual essentialism
  agency and, 10
  anti-, 7, 7n9, 39, 57

biologism equated with,
  58
feminist theory on, 4, 7–10,
  7nn6–9
race, 97–104
relational properties, 105
social context and, 104–5
taxonomy, 5–13
Ethics
  Aristotelian, 85, 86, 86n4, 91
  feminist theories of, 122,
    123n8
  Ruddick's material ethics, 63
Ethical identity
  biological identity
    distinguished from, 22,
    22n18
  person and, 58
Ethical normativity,
  76, 116
Ethical self, Appiah's, 23
Ethnic identity, 52
Evaluable under, 33
Exclusion argument, 8, 9

Feminist politics, 47, 125,
  127–32
Feminist theory
  anti-essentialism
    arguments, 7, 7n9, 39, 57
  essentialism in, 4, 7–10,
    7nn6–9
  ethics in, 63, 122, 123n8
  gender essentialism in,
    57–58, 57nn9–10, 67

Societies, human
engendering function as
necessary to, 100, 101–2
food production in, 100
gender-specific social
positions varying
among, 93
height, 27–29, 33
organizing of, 104
racialized, 98–101
Sortal properties, 21
Soul, 13
The Sources of Normativity
(Korsgaard), 114n5
Sperm and egg, 22–23
Standpoint and perspective
metaphor, 113–16
Statue analogy, 69–70, 72–73,
119
Stoljar, Natalie, 25–26
Synchronic unity, 79, 85,
87, 91

Taliban, 46
Taxonomy, essentialism,
5, 5n2
Theories. *See also* Feminist
theory
causal theory of
meaning, 51n2
relational theory of
self, 120–21
To do lists, 85
Transgendered individuals,
40–41, 41n9, 88, 88n7

Trauma victims, 121–22
Trinity, 57
dualistic ontology
distinguished from,
66–69, 66n18
ontology of self
and, 117–21

Uniessentialism, 4, 6, 10–11
application of, 15, 16,
16n14
feminist politics and, 128
functional essence and, 75
gender, 13–20, 104–6
kind essentialism
independence from,
12–13, 15–16
kind essentialism
interconnection with, 11
modal claims issue
for, 21n17
relational properties
and, 104
social individual, 30, 52–53
Unification essentialism. *See*
Uniessentialism
Unity. *See also* Normative unity
accidental unities
doctrine, 70n22
agents', 110, 112–14
of self, 117, 120
social individual, 78–79
synchronic and
diachronic, 79, 85,
87, 91

CPSIA information can be obtained at www.ICGtesting.com
Printed in the USA
BVOW04s1557131214

379096BV00001B/3/P